Stories for a Teen's Heart

Other Books compiled by Alice Gray

Stories for the Heart
More Stories for the Heart
Christmas Stories for the Heart
Stories for the Family Heart
Stories for a Woman's Heart
Stories for a Man's Heart
Stories for the Faithful Heart (January 2000)

Keepsakes for the Heart—Mothers
Keepsakes for the Heart—Friendship
Keepsakes for the Heart—Love
Keepsakes for the Heart—Faith

(*Keepsakes for the Heart* is an elegant gift collection that includes a hardbound book, complementary bookmark, note cards, and a charming box for keepsakes.)

What teens are saying about this book

Forget about all the bad news and get a dose of sunshine on a cloudy day. This is a teen's treasure of stories about best friends, loving family, kind-hearted strangers, and everyday heroes. Stories that will encourage you, make you laugh, look deep inside yourself, and leave you feeling good. Teens, this touch-your-heart book is definitely for us!

SHANNA STROEBEL
AGE 15

Stories for a Teen's Heart is about real-life struggles and joys. I laughed, cried, was encouraged, understood, and "lived" with the people in the stories. There are so many different subjects that everyone will find something to relate to his or her own life. I recommend this book to any teenager who needs encouragement, advice, a laugh, or just good stories that touch the heart.

DANAE JACOBSON
AGE 15

The stories were very good. Some brought a tear to my eye and others made me laugh.

HEATHER SCHWARZBURG
AGE 15

I think this book will speak well to teens' hearts. It covers all aspects of life in an encouraging way. From friends to truth, from love to hard times; it relates various lessons through stories in a user-friendly format.

SARAH MCGHEHEY
AGE 17

This book has stories that apply to everyday life from real people— it is a must read if you want to cry, laugh, and learn some lessons in life! I highly recommend this book for all teens! It applies to us all some way or another.

KRISTINA MCAULAY
AGE 15

The stories opened me to the realization that God's miracles aren't always huge; there are many small miracles that go unnoticed by people, yet they are the great ones.

JOHN ROBERTS
AGE 17

I feel that this book, just like the other books in the *Stories for the Heart* collection, will have a history of changing people's lives. Just reading these stories has changed the way I look at things. It has made me think about my actions, and it has brought back many memories. I hope that it touches other people's hearts as it has mine. These stories aren't just stories, they are real life. Thanks for the stories, Alice.

SHEENA LYNNELLE SHUCK
AGE 14

I really liked that I could relate to these stories. They are inspiring, funny, sad, and sweet.

ALLISON KNAPP
AGE 17

As I read the book, I felt as if I were standing at the scene of each story. The stories made me laugh and cry. They touched me and I believe they will also touch other teens.

STEPHANIE JOY HOWREY
AGE 16

This is an incredible compilation of excellent stories—stories that make you want to keep reading. Some of the stories are straight from the pen of people who were recently in the news and these people became more real. This was a highlight for me.

JEREMY MORRIS
AGE 14

Stories for a teen's Heart

COMPILED BY ALICE GRAY

Multnomah Publishers *Sisters, Oregon*

We have done our best to diligently seek reprint permission and provide accurate source attribution for all selections used in this book. However, if any attribution is found to be incorrect or lacking the proper permission license, the publisher welcomes notification and written documentation supporting corrections for subsequent printings. If you are, or know of, the proper copyright holder for any such story in this book, please contact us and we will properly credit and reimburse the contributor. We gratefully acknowledge the cooperation of other publishers and individuals for granting permission to use their material in this book. Please see the acknowledgment at the back of the book for complete attributions for this material.

STORIES FOR A TEEN'S HEART
published by Multnomah Publishers, Inc.

© 1999 by Alice Gray
International Standard Book Number: 1-57673-646-6

Cover photograph by Bob Jacobson/International Stock
Image on spine by Artbeats
Back cover photograph by Stephen Gardner
Interior illustrations by Elizabeth Haidle

Multnomah is a trademark of Multnomah Publishers, Inc.,
and is registered in the U.S. Patent and Trademark Office.
The colophon is a trademark of Multnomah Publishers, Inc.

Printed in the United States of America

For information:
MULTNOMAH PUBLISHERS, INC.•P. O. BOX 1720•SISTERS, OR 97759

Library of Congress Cataloging-in-Publication Data:
Stories for a teen's heart: over 100 stories to encourage a teen's
soul / compiled by Alice Gray.
    p. cm.
    ISBN 1-57673-646-6 (alk. paper)
    1. Teenagers—Religious life Anecdotes 2. Teenagers—Conduct of
life Anecdotes.   I. Gray, Alice, 1939–
BV4531.2.S83   1999
242'.63—dc21   99-40435
                                                    CIP

99 00 01 02 03 04 05 — 10 9 8 7 6 5 4 3 2 1

in celebration of —

TODAY'S TEENS
TOMORROW'S FUTURE

A Special Thank You

Jennifer Gates
for giving your heart and soul to this project.
You were God's special gift to me.

Cliff Boersma and Marlene Miller
for your devoted support during all the times we needed you.

Danae Jacobson, age fifteen,
for her creative writing. All quotes used on the divider pages were
selected from her essay, "Things I've Learned Lately."

Doreen Button, Casandra Lindell, and Tracy Sumner
for magical touches that made the stories more wonderful.

The authors
for sharing your hearts and lives and
for writing stories that honor teens.

Doreen Button, Robin Gerke, Aura Royer,
Lenette Stroebel, and Sauna Winsor
for extraordinary research.

Stephanie Howrey, Danae Jacobson, Allison Knapp,
Kristina McAulay, Sarah McGhehey, Jeremy Morris,
Rachel Neet, John Roberts, Heather Schwarzburg,
Sheena Lynnelle Shuck, Shanna Stroebel, and Mary Tennesen
for your teen perspective and inspiration.

My dear husband, Al
for always cheering me on.

Contents

Family

Inspiration

Good Times

Making a Difference

Changing

Faith

Acknowledgments

Family

Things I've Learned Lately...

Looking people in the eyes is showing them respect,
My grandma is my friend,
Memories are a treasure you should never let go,
And I never want to get too big for a hug from my dad.

Love's Sacrifice

KATHI KINGMA

Going to an affluent high school wasn't easy. I watched with envy as many of the "rich" kids drove their parents' sports cars and bragged about where they *bought* their designer clothes. I knew there was never a chance for me to compete with their wealthy status, but I also knew that it was a near crime if you wore the same outfit twice in the same month.

Coming from a family of five, with a tight budget, allowed us little hope for style. That didn't stop me from badgering my parents that I needed more fashionable clothes. My mother would frown at me. "Do you *need* them?"

"Yes," I would say adamantly. "I need them."

So shopping we would go. My mom waited outside the dressing room while I tried on the nicest clothes we could afford. I can recall several of these "necessity trips." Mom always went without complaining, never trying anything on for herself, though she'd look.

One day, when I was at home, I tried on one of my new outfits and modeled it in front of my parents' full-length mirror. As I was deciding what shoes looked best with the outfit, my eyes wandered to their closet, which was partially open. What I saw brought tears to my eyes. Three shirts hung on my mom's side of the closet. Three shirts that she'd worn endlessly and were old and faded. I pulled open the closet farther to see a few work shirts of my dad's that he'd worn for years. It had been ages since they bought anything for themselves, though their need was greater than mine.

That moment opened my eyes to see the sacrifices my parents had made over the years, sacrifices that showed me their love more powerfully than any words they could have said.

Nine Words

Never forget the nine most
important words of any family—
I love you.
You are beautiful.
Please forgive me.

—H. Jackson Brown, Jr.

Prom Date

SEAN COVEY
FROM *THE 7 HABITS OF HIGHLY EFFECTIVE TEENS*

When I was in ninth grade, my big brother Hans, who was a junior in high school, seemed to me to be the epitome of popularity. He was good in sports and dated a lot. Our house was always filled with his cool friends, guys I dreamed would some day think of me as something other than just "Hans's dumb little kid sister."

Hans asked Rebecca Knight, the most popular girl in the school, to go with him to the junior prom. She accepted. He rented the tux, bought the flowers, and, along with the rest of his popular crowd, hired a limo and made reservations at a fancy restaurant. Then, disaster struck. On the afternoon of the prom, Rebecca came down with a terrible strain of flu. Hans was without a date, and it was too late to ask another girl.

There were a number of ways Hans could have reacted, including getting angry, feeling sorry for himself, blaming Rebecca, even choosing to believe that she really wasn't sick and just didn't want go with him, in which case he would have had to believe that he was a loser. But Hans chose not only to remain positive but to give someone the night of her life.

He asked me! His little sister! To go with him to his junior prom.

Can you imagine my ecstasy? Mom and I flew about the house getting me ready. But when the limo pulled up with all of his friends, I almost chickened out. What would they think? But Hans just grinned, gave me his arm, and proudly escorted me out to the car like I was the queen of the ball. He didn't warn me not to act like a kid; he didn't apologize to the others; he ignored the fact that I was dressed in a simple short-skirted piano-recital dress while all of the other girls were in elegant formals.

I was bedazzled at the dance. Of course, I spilled punch on my dress. I'm sure Hans bribed every one of his friends to dance at least one dance with me, because I never sat out once. Some of them even pretended to fight over who got to dance with me. I had the greatest time. And so did Hans. While the guys were dancing with me he was dancing with their dates! The truth is, everyone was wonderful to me the whole night, and I think part of the reason was because Hans chose to be proud of me. It was the dream night of my life, and I think every girl in the school fell in love with my brother, who was cool enough, kind enough, and self-confident enough to take his little sister to his junior prom.

Grandma's Gift

WAYNE RICE
FROM *MORE HOT ILLUSTRATIONS FOR YOUTH TALK*

*A*s a ninth grader, Dave was the smallest kid in his high school. But at five feet tall and ninety pounds, he was the perfect candidate for the lightest weight class on the school's wrestling team.

Dave started out as the JV lightweight, but moved up to the varsity position when the boy at that spot moved away.

Unfortunately, Dave's first year was not one for the record books. Of the six varsity matches he wrestled, he was pinned six times.

Dave had a dream of someday being a good enough wrestler to receive his athlete's letter. An athlete's letter is a cloth emblem with the school's initials on it, which is awarded to those athletes who demonstrate exceptional performance in their sports. Those who were fortunate enough to receive a letter proudly wore it on their school letterman jackets.

Whenever Dave shared his dream of "lettering" in wrestling, most of his teammates and friends just laughed. Those who did offer encouragement to Dave usually said something like, "Well, it's not whether you win or lose..." or "It's not really important whether you letter or not...." Even so, Dave was determined to work hard and keep improving as a wrestler.

Every day after school, Dave was in the weight room trying to build up his strength, or running the stadium bleachers trying to increase his endurance, or in the wrestling room trying to improve his technique.

The one person who continually believed in Dave was his grandmother. Every time she saw him, she reminded him of what could be done through prayer and hard work. She told him to keep focused on his goal. Over and over again, she quoted Bible verses to him, like "I can do all things through Christ who gives me strength!" (Philippians 4:13).

The day before the next season began, Dave's grandmother passed away. He was heartbroken. If he ever did reach his goal of someday getting a high school letter, his grandmother would never know.

That season Dave's opponents faced a new person. What they expected was an easy victory. What they got instead was a ferocious battle. Dave won nine of his first ten matches that year.

Midway through the season, Dave's coach called him into his office to inform him that he would be receiving his high school letter. Dave was ecstatic. The only thing that could have made him feel better was to be able to share it with his grandmother. If only she knew!

Just then the coach smiled as he presented Dave with an envelope. The envelope had Dave's name written on it in his grandmother's handwriting. He opened it and read:

> Dear Dave,
>   I knew you could do it! I set aside $100 to buy you a school jacket to put your letter on. I hope you'll wear it proudly, and remember, "You can do all things through Christ who gives you strength!"
>
>   Congratulations,
>   Grandma

After Dave finished reading the letter, his coach reached behind him and pulled out a brand new jacket with the school letter attached and Dave's name embroidered on the front. Dave realized then that his grandmother did know after all.

Not All Valentines Come in Envelopes

ROBIN JONES GUNN

s a teenager, I worked as a waitress at a Coco's restaurant, in Southern California. Although California nights are supposed to be warm, on this particular February night the brisk wind shrieked through the front door. Around nine o'clock things slowed down and that's when I started feeling sorry for myself. You see, all my friends had gone to the movies, but I had to work until closing.

I didn't pay much attention to the man who entered the restaurant. A flurry of leaves followed him in. The sound of the wailing wind fell silent as the door shut itself. I busied myself making more coffee. Suddenly the hostess grabbed by arm. "This is really creepy," she whispered, "but there's a man with a white moustache over there who said he wouldn't eat here unless you were his waitress."

I swallowed hard. "Is he a weirdo?"

"See for yourself," she said.

We carefully peered through the decorative foliage at the mysterious man in the corner. Slowly he lowered his menu, revealing thick, white hair, silver-blue eyes, and a wide grin beneath his white moustache. He lifted his hand and waved.

"That's no weirdo!" I said. "That's my dad!"

"You mean he came to see you at work?" The hostess balked. "That's pretty strange, if you ask me."

I didn't think it was very strange. I thought it was kind of neat. But I didn't let Dad know that. Poor Dad! I acted so nonchalant, rattling off the soup of the day and scribbling down his order before anyone could see him squeeze my elbow and say, "Thanks, honey."

But I want you to know something—I never forgot that night. His being there said a thousand things to me. As he silently watched me clear tables and refill coffee cups, I could hear his unspoken words bouncing off the walls: "I'm here. I support you. I'm proud of you. You're doing a great job. Keep up the good work. You're my girl. I love you." It was the best valentine I received that year.

Stick Shift

CLARK COTHERN
FROM *AT THE HEART OF EVERY GREAT FATHER*

The day I drove a white, 1960 Ford pickup truck to high school, I had my eye on a cute little flute player who sat in the front row during band. Jeanie was fourteen and claimed to have "vast experience" driving a stick shift. I figured one way to impress a fourteen-year-old girl would be to let her drive "my" truck around the school parking lot. Jeanie became very excited about the possibility. I became very excited that she had become very excited. What a wonderful way to flood sunshine on a blossoming relationship.

Only two problems existed with this arrangement. First, "my" truck actually belonged to my dad. Second, the only thing "vast" about the girl's experience with stick shifts was the size of her imagination. Her actual logged *experience* with a stick shift, it turned out, amounted to one quick drive in somebody's VW Bug.

After my hasty explanation of which pedal did what, she followed my instructions and pushed in the clutch, extending her short little left leg as far as it would go. With her toes trembling, she held that pedal down.

23

With her other foot, she gently pressed on the gas pedal.

The old truck roared to life as she turned the key. As I had explained, she began slowly lifting up on the clutch with her left foot while at the same time slowly depressing the gas pedal with her right foot.

That's when the plan began to unravel.

Her footwork became a bit erratic when the clutch engaged and the truck lurched forward. She tried to cram her foot back down on the clutch pedal but forgot about her right foot, which was jammed down as hard as she could push...onto the accelerator.

Sitting in the middle of the wide seat, I watched little sections of the nearby shop-class building jerk by in the rearview mirror. I felt like a rodeo cowboy riding his first bucking bronco as the truck jerked forward in wild, untamed motions.

Trying to remain calm, I yelled, "It's okay!" Who was I kidding? With nothing to hold onto, I was lurching back and forth like wet jeans in an unbalanced spin cycle.

"Just push down on the clutch and let off the gas," I hollered above the noise of the engine, which was revving and dying in time to the jerking motions of the truck.

"Which one's the clutch?" she screamed back. I guess my lesson hadn't sunk in.

"The one on the left," I said.

"Is what?" she asked. "Which one is the brake?"

We really didn't have time for this conversation to be taking place since we were quickly running out of parking lot. Just about the time I thought to help her by grabbing the stick shift and yanking it into neutral, I noticed the chain-link fence looming dangerously close to our left and just ahead.

The fence wasn't what bothered me so much. It was the faculty parking lot filled with cars just *beyond* the fence that really got my heart racing.

Suddenly, before I had a chance to turn the key to "off" or to grab the steering wheel and turn it toward open space, I heard the sickening sound of metal against metal. Nice, straight, shiny-aluminum poles began bending like pipe cleaners as the Ford-pickup-turned-tank mowed down a healthy section of newly installed fence.

Finally, for lack of gas and momentum, the old truck stalled, and silence filled the cab. I noticed my friend's cute little legs trembling as she stood straight up on both pedals, with her knuckles white and locked onto the steering wheel.

"Well," I said, breathing for the first time in several agonizing seconds, "that wasn't so bad, for a first try."

She crawled over my lap onto the passenger side of the truck while I surveyed the damage from the window. I couldn't believe what I was looking at. The bumper of the heavy old truck was resting less than twelve inches away from the bumper of the vice principal's Buick Regal.

My heart finished the bossa nova and returned to regular rhythm again, and I decided to own up to the experience. I backed the truck into an actual parking space, thanked my young friend for a lovely time, and excused myself to the vice principal's office.

Maryvale High School in Phoenix was quite large at the time since Trevor Brown High was still under construction to our west. So, with five thousand kids to handle, our principal, David Goodson only dealt with really major issues like riots and gun control. The vice president, a.k.a. "No Mercy" Miller, was the guy who got to hear all the really good stories...like the one I told him.

I took full responsibility for my actions and for driving the truck into the fence, feeling a bit unsettled by the wide, silly grin on his face the whole time.

When I finished my tale of woe, Mr. Miller said, "Tell you what you do. Call this number," and he handed me a business card. On it was the name and phone number of a fence company.

"They just installed the fence you ran into...*yesterday.*"

My knees grew weak. It was at that very moment I realized just how fortunate I had been. If that wonderful fence hadn't been there to stop our forward progress—like a cable stopping jets on an aircraft carrier—we would have nailed Mr. M's Buick but good!

He continued, "Tell the owner what happened, and see if he'll let you pay for the damages out of your own pocket. Since this happened on private property, we won't have to call the police for an accident report."

Sigh. Ah, at that moment I could have almost kissed that man. Almost. The V.P. could have given me what I really deserved—or worse—but instead, he gently helped me learn my lesson and take responsibility for my actions. He remained absolutely calm through the entire ordeal.

I called the name on the card, and a very kind man answered, "Oh yeah, heard about that little incident." I didn't know if he was loud because he was shouting over machinery noise or if he always talked like that. "I'm a little surprised to hear from you," he shouted. "One of my installers called me with the details. Says he was able to bend back three of the four posts you knocked down. The fourth one snapped like a toothpick. Why don't you come down here to my office and pay me...oh, say, ten bucks for the pipe, and we'll be back in business."

All the way down to his office I was repeating, "Thank You, God. Oh, thank You, thank You, thank You!"

With that taken care of, I faced the most difficult part of this trial. I still had to break the news to my dad.

I parked the truck as far up in the driveway as I could, with the left front fender facing away from the house. When Dad arrived home from work, I caught him as he was stepping out of the car, so I could set the right mood.

"Hey, Dad, how was work?" I acted really friendly. Maybe a tad too friendly.

"Just fine, Son. What's up?" He must have been able to tell by the way I was shifting my weight from side to side that I was a little hyped. That and the fact that my voice was up to an E-flat.

"Well, Dad, you'll never guess what happened today at school. The funniest thing." I laughed, mostly out of pure nervous energy but also hoping he would catch it and laugh with me, at least just a little.

Using the most animated and humorous expressions I could muster, I explained in detail, from start to finish, the entire episode to my father; including the fact that the vice principal had worn that silly grin on his face the whole time I was telling him my story. Then I said, "Kinda like that one you've got on your face right now, Dad!" And I laughed some more.

He sighed, chuckled, shook his head from side to side, and then put his hand on my shoulder and said, "Let's take a look at the truck."

I tried to find enough saliva in my mouth to swallow as we walked around to the damaged fender and surveyed the scratches. They weren't that bad, considering what it'd been through that day. Those old trucks were really built. He looked at the damage, sighed one more time, and then said, "You know what happened to me and one of my brothers when I was about your age?"

Suddenly I was able to swallow. I had heard his sermons before, but I figured being preached at was better than some other forms of punishment he might have devised. I acted really interested.

He said, "Your uncle and I found an old truck that belonged to our dad, your grandfather. We decided to surprise him by getting the truck down the hill, into the barn, and back into working order."

(This was getting interesting. Better than most of the sermons I'd heard before.)

"Well, it wasn't until we got the old truck rolling downhill that we made a very important discovery. There were no brakes. In this instance it wasn't a chain-link fence that stopped the truck. It was a 4-inch by 4-inch fence post."

I caught myself gawking just a bit, so I closed my mouth, which had opened as Dad revealed this compelling truth about his boyhood. Not as fearful as I was before his story, I awaited sentencing.

Dad said, "I suppose that if you sand this area, first with a coarse grit and then with a fine one, we could probably match that color pretty well with a store-bought spray and just touch it up a little. This is an old truck, after all."

It had been a hat-trick day for gentleness. Three times in one day I had not been yelled at. Not once.

First the vice principal, then the man at the fence place, and now my dad. I almost couldn't believe this was happening. I followed Dad's advice, and in no time at all we had the old truck back in nearly good-as-used shape. The whole day had been a terrific learning experience for me: telling the truth to the vice principal, paying for the fence, helping with the bodywork on the truck, and all the while absorbing an even more valuable lesson in the process.

I learned that day about gentleness and about teaching lessons to sons who make mistakes. Dad's message sank in deep because he combined strength with gentleness. The gentleness softened the shell around my heart and allowed the arrow of truth to pierce right into its target.

The best way to keep kids at home is to make the home a pleasant atmosphere...and to let the air out of their tires.

—Author unknown

Love Letters to My Unborn Child

JUDITH HAYES
FROM *FOCUS ON THE FAMILY* MAGAZINE

I t was a balmy summer day in late July. I had been feeling rather queasy and nauseated, so I decided to see my doctor.

"Mrs. Hayes, I'm happy to tell you that you are ten weeks pregnant," my doctor announced. I couldn't believe my ears. It was a dream come true.

My husband and I were young and had been married for only a year. We were working hard to build a happy life together. The news that we were expecting a baby was exciting and scary.

In my youthful enthusiasm I decided to write "love letters" to our baby to express my feelings of expectancy and joy. Little did I know just how valuable those love letters would be in years to come.

August 1971: Oh, my darling baby, can you feel the love I have for you while you are so small and living in the quiet world inside my body? Your daddy and I want the world to be perfect for you with no hate, no wars, no pollution. I can't wait to hold you in my arms in just six months! I love you, and Daddy loves you but he can't feel you yet.

September 1971: I am four months pregnant and am feeling better. I can tell you are growing, and I hope you are well and comfortable. I've been taking vitamins and eating healthy foods for you. Thank goodness my morning sickness is gone. I think about you all the time.

October 1971: Oh, these melancholy moods. I cry so often over so little. Sometimes I feel very alone, and then I remember you are growing inside of me. I feel you stirring, now tumbling and turning and pushing. It's never the same. Your movements always bring me so much joy!

November 1971: I am feeling much better now that my fatigue and nausea have passed. The intense heat of summer is over. The weather is lovely, crisp and breezy. I feel your movements often now. Constant punching and kicking. What elation to know you are alive and well. Last week Daddy and I heard your strong heartbeat at the doctor's office.

February 2, 1972 at 11:06 P.M.: You were born! We named you Sasha. It was a long, hard twenty-two hour labor, and your daddy helped me relax and stay calm. We are so happy to see you, to hold you, and to greet you. Welcome, our firstborn child. We love you so much!

Sasha was soon one year old and cautiously toddling all over the house. Then she was riding ponies and swinging in the sunshine at the park. Our little blue-eyed beauty entered kindergarten and grew into a bright and strong-willed little girl. The years passed so quickly that my husband and I joked that we put our five-year-old daughter to bed one night and she woke up the next morning as a teenager.

Those few years of adolescence and rebellion were not easy. There were times my beautiful yet angry teenager would dig her feet into the ground and yell, "I hate you! You never loved me! You don't care about me or want me to be happy!"

Her harsh words cut at my heart. What could I have done wrong?

After one of my daughter's angry outbursts, I suddenly remembered the little box of love letters tucked away in my bedroom closet. I found them and quietly placed them on her bed, hoping she would read them. A few days later, she appeared before me with tears in her eyes.

"Mom, I never knew just how much you truly loved me—even before I was born!" she said. "How could you love me without knowing me? You loved me unconditionally!" That very precious moment became a bond of unity that still exists between us today. Those dusty old love letters melted away the anger and rebellion she had been feeling.

Mom's Note

I know you are angry with me.
But don't forget for a second that I love you.
No matter what you do, or say, or think,
you can always depend on my support and love.
I love you,
Mom

—*from* P.S. I Love You

Christmas Day in the Morning

PEARL S. BUCK

He waked suddenly and completely. It was four o'clock, the hour at which his father had always called him to get up and help with the milking. Strange how the habits of his youth clung to him still! Fifty years ago, and his father had been dead for thirty years, and yet he waked at four o'clock in the morning. He had trained himself to turn over and go to sleep, but this morning, because it was Christmas, he did not try to sleep.

He slipped back in time, as he did so easily nowadays. He was fifteen years old and still on his father's farm. He loved his father. He had not known it until one day a few days before Christmas, when he overheard what his father was saying to his mother.

"Mary, I hate to call Rob in the mornings. He's growing so fast, and he needs his sleep. If you could see how he sleeps when I go in to wake him up! I wish I could manage alone."

"Well, you can't, Adam." His mother's voice was brisk. "Besides, he isn't a child anymore. It's time he took his turn."

"Yes," his father said slowly. "But I sure do hate to wake him."

When he heard those words, something in him woke: his father loved him! He had never thought of it before, taking for granted the tie of their blood. Neither his father nor his mother talked about loving their children—they had no time for such things. There was always so much to do on a farm.

Now that he knew his father loved him, there would be no more loitering in the mornings and having to be called again. He got up after that, stumbling with sleep, and pulled on his clothes, his eyes shut, but he got up.

And then on the night before Christmas, that year when he was fifteen, he lay for a few minutes thinking about the next day. They were poor, and most of the excitement was in the turkey they had raised themselves and in the mince pies his mother made. His sisters sewed presents and his mother and father always bought something he needed, not only a warm jacket, maybe, but something more, such as a book. And he saved and bought them each something, too.

He wished, that Christmas he was fifteen, he had a better present for his father. As usual, he had gone to the ten-cent store and bought a tie. It had seemed nice enough until he lay thinking the night before Christmas, and then he wished that he had heard his father and mother talking in time for him to save for something better.

He lay on his side, his head supported by his elbow, and looked out of his attic window. The stars were bright, much brighter than he ever remembered them being, and one was so bright he wondered if it were really the star of Bethlehem.

"Dad," he had once asked when he was a little boy, "what is a stable?"

"It's just a barn," his father had replied, "like ours."

Then Jesus had been born in a barn, and to a barn the shepherds and the Wise Men had come, bringing their Christmas gifts!

The thought struck him like a silver dagger. Why should he not give his father a special gift, too, out there in the barn? He could get up early, earlier than four o'clock, and he could creep into the barn and get all the milking done. He'd do it alone, milk and clean up, and then when his father went in to start the milking, he'd see it all done. And he would know who had done it.

At a quarter to three, he got up and put on his clothes. He crept downstairs, careful of the creaky boards, and let himself out. The big star hung lower over the barn roof, a reddish gold. The cows looked at him, sleepy and surprised.

"So, boss," he whispered. They accepted him placidly, and he fetched some hay for each cow and then got the milking pail and the big milk cans.

He had never milked all alone before, but it seemed almost easy. He kept thinking about his father's surprise. His father would come in and call him, saying that he would get things started while Rob was getting dressed. He'd go to the barn, open the door, and then he'd go to get the two big empty milk cans. But they wouldn't be waiting or empty; they'd be standing in the milk house filled.

The task went more easily than he had ever known it to before. Milking for once was not a chore. It was something else, a gift to his father who loved him. He finished, the two milk cans were full, and he covered them and closed the milk house door carefully, making sure of the latch. He put the stool in its place by the door and hung up the clean milk pail. Then he went out of the barn and barred the door behind him.

Back in his room, he had only a minute to pull off his clothes in the darkness and jump into bed, for he heard his father up. He put the covers over his head to silence his quick breathing. The door opened.

"Rob!" his father called. "We have to get up, son, even if it is Christmas."

"Aw-right," he said sleepily.

"I'll go on out," his father said. "I'll get things started."

The door closed and he lay still, laughing to himself. In just a few minutes his father would know. His dancing heart was ready to jump from his body.

The minutes were endless—ten, fifteen, he did not know how many—and he heard his father's steps again. The door opened and he lay still.

"Rob!"

"Yes, Dad—"

His father was laughing, a queer sobbing sort of laugh. "Thought you'd fool me did you?" His father was standing beside him, pulling away the cover.

"It's for Christmas, Dad!"

He found his father and clutched him in a great hug. He felt his father's arms go around him. It was dark, and they could not see each other's faces.

"Son, I thank you. Nobody ever did a nicer thing—"

"Oh, Dad, I want you to know—I do want to be good!" The words broke from him of their own will. He did not know what to say. His heart was bursting with love.

"Well, I reckon I can go back to bed and sleep," his father said after a moment. "No, hark—the little ones are waked up. Come to think of it, son, I've never seen you children when you first saw the Christmas tree. I was always in the barn. Come on!"

Rob got up and pulled on his clothes again, and they went down to the Christmas tree; and soon the sun was creeping up where the star had been. Oh, what a Christmas, and how his heart had nearly burst again with shyness and pride as his father told his mother and made the younger children listen about how he, Rob, had gotten up all by himself.

"The best Christmas gift I ever had and I'll remember it, son, every year on Christmas morning, so long as I live."

They both remembered it, and now that his father was dead he remembered it alone: that blessed Christmas dawn when, alone with the cows in the barn, he had made his first gift of true love.

Love Wins

Patsy G. Lovell
CONDENSED FROM FOCUS ON THE FAMILY MAGAZINE

When our daughter Kathleen was thirteen, she was a lively teenager. One day, she excitedly asked permission to buy a short leather skirt, one like all the other girls in her class were wearing.

I could tell she was expecting a negative response. Nonetheless, she acted surprised when I said no, then launched into great detail how she would be the only one in the class without a leather skirt. I again said no and explained my reasons.

"Well, I think you're wrong!" she retorted.

"Wrong or right, I've made the decision. The answer is no."

Kathleen stomped off, but quickly turned on her heels. "I just want to explain why this is so important to me. If I don't have this skirt, I'll be left out. And all my friends won't like me."

"The answer is no," I quietly repeated.

She puffed up like a balloon and played her final card. "I thought you loved me," she wailed.

"I do. But the answer is still no." With that, she "whumped"—a noise made only by an angry junior high kid trying to get her way. She ran upstairs and slammed her bedroom door.

Even though I had won the battle, I felt I was losing the war. Then an unexplainable thing happened: an inner voice said *Hold fast!*

The whumping noise started once more, and Kathleen appeared on the stairs. This time, she was breathing fire.

"I thought you taught us that we have rights!" she screamed.

"You do have rights. The answer is still no."

She wound up again, but I cut her off. "Kathleen, I have made my decision. I will not change my mind, and if you say another word about this you will be severely punished. Now go to bed!"

She still had a few words left, but she held them in check. Visibly seething, she disappeared.

I sat on the couch, shaking and upset. Since my husband was working late, I was the only parent "on duty." None of the children had ever pushed me so far. Just when I thought our skirmishes were over, I heard it again—whumping. Kathleen came down the stairs.

"Well," she announced, "I'm just going to tell you one more time…"

I met her at the bottom step, planted my hands on my hips, and looked her in the eyes. "Do not answer," I said. "Do not say anything. Turn around and go to bed. Without a single sound!"

For several minutes I stared into space and wondered what my blood pressure was. Then I heard her door open. Kathleen, her nose and eyes red from crying, walked down the stairs in pajamas and curlers. She held out her arms to me.

"Oh, Mom, I'm sorry."

We hugged as she said though her tears, "I was so scared!"

"Scared of what?" I asked.

"I was scared that you were going to let me win!" she sniffed.

You were scared that I was going to let you win? I was confused for a moment. Then I realized my daughter had wanted *me* to win!

I had done the right thing—Kathleen's simple words assured me. I had held fast, and now she was holding onto me.

A Father, a Son and an Answer

BOB GREENE
FROM CHICAGO TRIBUNE

Passing through the Atlanta airport one morning, I caught one of those trains that take travelers from the main terminal to their boarding gates. Free, sterile, and impersonal, the trains run back and forth all day long. Not many people consider them fun, but on this Saturday I heard laughter.

At the front of the first car—looking out the window at the track that lay ahead—were a man and his son. We had just stopped to let off passengers, and the doors were closing again. "Here we go! Hold on to me tight," the father said. The boy, about five years old, made sounds of sheer delight.

Most people on the train were dressed for business trips or vacations—and the father and son were dressed in clothes that were just about as inexpensive as you can buy.

"Look out there!" the father said to his son. "See that pilot? I bet he's walking to his plane." The son craned his neck to look.

As I got off, I remembered something I'd wanted to buy in the terminal.

I was early for my flight, so I decided to go back. I did—and just as I was about to reboard the train for my gate, I saw that the man and his son had returned too. I realized then that they hadn't been heading for a flight, but had just been riding the shuttle.

"You want to go home now?" the father asked.

"I want to ride some more!"

"More?" the father said, mock-exasperated but clearly pleased. "You're not tired?"

"This is fun!" his son said.

"All right," the father replied, and when a door opened we all got on.

There are parents who can afford to send their children to Europe or Disneyland, and the children turn out rotten. There are parents who live in million-dollar houses and give their children cars and swimming pools, yet something goes wrong. Rich and poor, black and white, so much goes wrong so often.

"Where are all these people going, Daddy?" the son asked.

"All over the world," came the reply. The other people in the airport were leaving for distant destinations or arriving at the ends of their journeys. The father and son, though, were just riding this shuttle together, making it exciting, sharing each other's company.

So many troubles in this country—so many questions about what to do.

The answer is so simple: parents who care enough to spend time, and to pay attention, and try their best. It doesn't cost a cent, yet it is the most valuable thing in the world.

The train picked up speed, and the father pointed something out, and the boy laughed again, and the answer is so simple.

Come Home

Max Lucado
FROM *No Wonder They Call Him the Savior*

The small house was simple but adequate. It consisted of one large room on a dusty street. Its red-tiled roof was one of many in this poor neighborhood on the outskirts of the Brazilian village. It was a comfortable home. Maria and her daughter, Christina, had done what they could to add color to the gray walls and warmth to the hard dirt floor: an old calendar, a faded photograph of a relative, a wooden crucifix. The furnishings were modest: a pallet on either side of the room, a washbasin, and a wood-burning stove.

Maria's husband had died when Christina was an infant. The young mother, stubbornly refusing opportunities to remarry, got a job and set out to raise her young daughter. And now, fifteen years later, the worst years were over. Though Maria's salary as a maid afforded few luxuries, it was reliable and it did provide food and clothes. And now Christina was old enough to get a job to help out.

Some said Christina got her independence from her mother. She recoiled at the traditional idea of marrying young and raising a family. Not that she couldn't have had her pick of husbands. Her olive skin and brown eyes kept a steady stream of prospects at her door. She had an infectious way of throwing her head back and filling the room with laughter. She also had that rare magic some women have that makes every man feel like a king just by being near them. But it was her spirited curiosity that made her keep all the men at arm's length.

She spoke often of going to the city. She dreamed of trading her dusty neighborhood for exciting avenues and city life. Just the thought of this horrified her mother. Maria was always quick to remind Christina of the harshness of the streets. "People don't know you there. Jobs are scarce and the life is cruel. And besides, if you went there, what would you do for a living?"

Maria knew exactly what Christina would do, or would have to do for a living. That's why her heart broke when she awoke one morning to find her daughter's bed empty. Maria knew immediately where her daughter had gone. She also knew immediately what she must do to find her. She quickly threw some clothes in a bag, gathered up all her money, and ran out of the house.

On her way to the bus stop she entered a drugstore to get one last thing. Pictures. She sat in the photograph booth, closed the curtain, and spent all she could on pictures of herself. With her purse full of small black-and-white photos, she boarded the next bus to Rio de Janeiro.

Maria knew Christina had no way of earning money. She also knew that her daughter was too stubborn to give up. When pride meets hunger, a human will do things that were before unthinkable. Knowing this, Maria began her search. Bars, hotels, night clubs, any place with the reputation for street walkers or prostitutes. She went to them all. And at each place she left her picture—taped on a bathroom mirror, tacked to a hotel bulletin board, fastened to a corner phone booth. And on the back of each photo she wrote a note.

It wasn't too long before both the money and the pictures ran out, and Maria had to go home. The weary mother wept as the bus began its long journey back to her small village.

It was a few weeks later that young Christina descended the hotel stairs. Her young face was tired. Her brown eyes no longer danced with youth but spoke of pain and fear. Her laughter was broken. Her dream had become a nightmare. A thousand times over she had longed to trade these countless beds for her secure pallet. Yet the little village was, in too many ways, too far away.

As she reached the bottom of the stairs, her eyes noticed a familiar face. She looked again, and there on the lobby mirror was a small picture of her mother. Christina's eyes burned and her throat tightened as she walked across the room and removed the small photo. Written on the back was this compelling invitation. "Whatever you have done, whatever you have become, it doesn't matter. Please come home."

She did.

A Different Kind of Tears

SUNDI ARRANTS
AGE 18

t was my freshman year of high school and everything was going great in my life. I was in a large school and my biggest worry was getting lost on my way to the next class.

Then one day everything changed.

My family's seemingly perfect life was shattered. My dad woke up in the middle of the night with a horrible pain in his side. We rushed him to the hospital and tests revealed he had cancer. The doctors told us Dad would be in the hospital for a long time. They started him on chemotherapy and he felt even worse from the treatments.

The hospital was quite a distance from home and since I was in school, I could only see him on the weekends. Every day I made a get well card and Mom delivered it for me. I missed him terribly and slept with his picture under my pillow. Sometimes when I couldn't sleep, I held the picture close to my heart and cried.

Finally Dad was allowed to come home from the hospital, but he still had to go back twice a week for his chemotherapy treatments. He was very pale and each day he seemed to get worse. The chemotherapy made his hair fall out a little at a time.

I'll never forget the day I came home from school and my dad was wearing a baseball cap. He took it off and asked me what I thought of his new haircut. So much of his hair had fallen out, he had decided to have it completely shaved off.

I didn't want to hurt his feelings, so I told him I loved it and that he looked really cool. But in my heart, I could hardly stand to see him looking that way.

There was another day I'll never forget. A few weeks later my parents sat down with me and told me tearfully and solemnly that Dad would probably not live much longer. I can't describe that awful moment. It was like some wild beast was raking its claws across my heart. It hit me that my dad would not be there to see me graduate from high school. He wouldn't be there to walk me down the aisle when I married. He would never hold my children in his arms.

I was crushed and it seemed like something died inside me. I thought, *How can I go on with my life when Dad is losing his?*

My oldest brother, who was still a teenager, did his best to shoulder the load as "dad" in our home. My little brother was too young to understand what was going on. But my mother, who is the best friend I have in the whole world, did everything she could to encourage us about Dad. Although her own heart was breaking, she never gave up hoping for a miracle. No matter how much she was hurting inside, she was there for my dad and for my brothers and me. How she did it, I don't know. I guess only a mother knows that secret.

After many months something wonderful happened. Our prayers were answered—Dad was getting better. Dad's hair began to grow back. Color was returning to his face and he was smiling again. The whole world seemed brighter. We watched as God took our shattered lives and hearts and put them back together again—one piece at a time.

Recently I graduated from high school. As I stood before friends and their families to give the salutatorian address, I looked out in the audience and saw my dad sitting beside Mom. There were tears in his eyes, and I thought of the day he told me he might not live to see me graduate. But these were different tears—tears of happiness and love. The same kind of tears he will shed the day he walks me down the aisle at my wedding.

Because

ADRIA DOBKIN
GRADUATION SPEECH
MOUNTAIN VIEW HIGH SCHOOL

My mother started playing the cello when she was forty-six years old. She had always wanted to learn how to play, and finally, as a middle-aged mother of two teenagers, she decided to take lessons.

I listened to her scratch out "Twinkle Twinkle Little Star," and slowly progress to more challenging pieces. To say I wasn't her biggest fan is an understatement.

She would come to me with her frustrations, wanting to quit, and I wouldn't say anything. I wasn't very supportive.

It seemed to me a waste. Playing the cello wasn't something my mother could put on her college applications. She was never going to play with the London Symphony Orchestra. I didn't see the point.

But my mother's point was not to please admissions officers or wow her peers. She did it just because.

It's this strive for internal self-improvement that leads to a sort of glow. Knowing that you have done something special for no other reason but "because."

"IT's A letter from his son in college... and he's
not asking for any money..."

A Father's Blessing

MORGAN CRYAR
FROM *DECISION* MAGAZINE

Many a morning as a child I stumbled through the darkness to our family's truck, fell back to sleep, then was awakened by the sound of the truck sputtering to a halt in the Louisiana woods. I can remember, even when I was too young to dress myself, climbing out of that truck alongside my dad—the most important person in my life at the time—and stepping into the gray, early morning light to hunt squirrels or deer.

One morning ten years ago I was once again headed for the woods to hunt with Dad. But this time I was grown, with a family of my own. I had been touring for months and had promised to make a trip from our home in Nashville, Tennessee, to the swamps outside Lake Charles, Louisiana, where I had grown up. Though I didn't know it, this would be no ordinary morning. It was the morning that I would find out that Dad approved. This morning he would give me his blessing.

When we got into Dad's old truck and he turned the ignition key, music began to pour from a cassette in the tape deck. I knew the music well and was surprised to hear it in Dad's truck. It was my most recent recording, blaring into the morning stillness! I couldn't help myself; I said, "I didn't know you even had this. Do you listen to it?"

His answer amazed me. "It's the only thing I listen to." I glanced around, and sure enough, it was the only cassette in his truck. I was dumbstruck! He said, "This is my favorite," referring to the song playing at the time. I let his words sink in as he turned down the volume to match the morning.

We drove in silence down the road toward the hunting spot, and I wondered at what had just happened. It seems now like such a small thing—a few spoken words. But there seemed to be something different in the air. I sat taller in my seat. I looked at my dad out of the corner of my eye and thought back to two turning points in our relationship.

One turning point happened while I was in college. I remembered having it dawn on me that I had never heard my dad say that he loved me. I knew that he did, but I couldn't remember having heard him say so. That was something my dad just didn't do. For some reason it became important to me that I hear those words from his own lips. I knew, however, that he would never initiate it. So that summer, as I drove home from college, I determined to "force his hand" by telling him first that I loved him. Then he'd have to say it back. It would be simple. Just three little words. I anticipated a glorious new openness once I came home and said, "I love you, Dad," and then he would respond.

But simple is not always easy. The first day came and went, and I thought, "I have to tell him tomorrow!" The next day came and went. Then the next, and the next. Then twelve weeks passed, and it was the last day of my summer break. I was frustrated at not having said those three little words to my dad.

My little, beat-up car was packed and sitting on the gravel driveway. I promised myself that I would not start the engine until the deed was done. To someone with an emotionally open relationship with his own father, this may all seem a bit silly, but to me it was serious business. My palms were wet and my throat was dry. My knees grew weak as departure time came.

It had been a good summer visit. There was a general sadness in the house because I was headed back to school across the state. Finally I could wait no longer. I hugged my mom, my brother, and my sister good-bye, and went back to find my dad.

I walked up to him, looked him in the eyes and said, "I love you, Dad."

He smiled a half smile, put his arms around me and said what I needed to hear: "I love you too, son." It seemed as though a thousand volts of electricity were in the air as we hugged each other (another thing that hadn't happened since I was a small child). It was such a little thing, but it changed everything!

From that point on, all of our conversations were signed off with: "I love you, Dad." "I love you too, son." It became commonplace to embrace when we greeted each other and when we parted. As plain as it sounds, it resulted in a new sweetness between my dad and me. The memory of it came back to me in the truck that morning on the way to the woods.

The other turning point came after college. I remembered that I had learned at a seminar about clearing my conscience with those whom I had wronged. This was entirely new to me—admitting guilt and receiving forgiveness from those I had offended.

Part of the process was to ask God to show me anyone and everyone with whom I needed to clear my conscience. Sure enough, at the top of the list was Dad.

So I sat down with my dad and started first with the worst things that I had done. I proceeded from there to the least serious offenses. I confessed everything that I knew had hurt him, even from my childhood. Then I simply asked, "Dad, will you forgive me?"

Just as I had expected, Dad was embarrassed and tried to shrug it off: "Aw, it's all right, son."

I said, "It will mean a lot to me if you will forgive me."

He looked right at me and said, "It has already been forgiven."

That was his way of saying that he had not held a grudge. And once again, everything changed. From that moment Dad treated me with new respect. I hadn't anticipated it, but he also began to treat me like an adult—like a friend.

In the stillness of the morning, on the way to the woods, these things floated through my memory, and I rested in my dad's approval of my calling, my work, my music.

I had no way of knowing just how precious his blessing would become to me. One short week later, after my family and I had driven back to Nashville, I received the telephone call from my brother, Tommy, telling me that Dad had walked out onto the porch and had died of a heart attack. He had been young and healthy—only forty-nine years old. It was my darkest day.

Though my family and I tasted intense grief, I still had much for which to be grateful. I had enjoyed thirty years with my dad—some of them as his friend. He had given me a strong enough start that I knew I could meet the challenge of rearing my own children, including my son who was born on Father's Day six years later.

Even though my dad is gone, in the wee hours of that morning on the way to the woods, he had given me something of great value to pass along—a father's blessing.

inspiration

Things I've Learned Lately...

*Books are like friends who share
a little of themselves with you,
Change is inevitable,
Chocolate-chip cookies taste better as dough,
And you should never wait to tell
someone why you love them.*

Triumph Over Tragedy

VALEEN SCHNURR
AGE 18
AS TOLD TO JANNA L. GRABER

Graduation day was a sweltering Saturday afternoon in May. Sitting with four hundred of my classmates in an outdoor amphitheater, I was hot in my cap and gown.

I had looked forward to this day for months. The past four years at Columbine High School in Littleton, Colorado, had gone quickly. My days had been filled with studies, work as a peer counselor, school clubs, and lots of time with my friends. Today we were celebrating our accomplishments. We were celebrating life.

I listened as speaker after speaker came to the podium, speaking of the future, remembering the past. A loud foghorn sounded in the audience, and I grinned as a beach ball was tossed from person to person across the crowd. For a moment—just a moment—this graduation day seemed almost like the day I had envisioned.

Then I watched as the parents of my friend, Lauren Townsend, made their way across the stage. With pride on their faces, they accepted a diploma for Lauren, a class valedictorian. And once again, I realized how much things had changed since that awful day four weeks before.

My life, and the lives of thousands of others, had changed on April 20, 1999. I had just gone to the library that morning. As was custom that semester, I met five other girls from English class there. Sometimes we worked on studies; other times we just talked.

I sat down to read a new book for peer counseling, while my friends sat nearby working on an English project. Then suddenly, a teacher came running into the library. "Everyone get down!" she screamed. "There's a kid with a gun!"

At first my friends and I thought it must be a senior prank. Then, from the floor beneath us, we heard the sound of screaming and gunfire. The floor shook as bombs went off below our feet. My friends and I dove beneath a table. I was closest to Lauren. In fear, we grasped hands, clutching each other tightly. I began to pray silently, begging God to help us.

"It'll be okay," Lauren said over and over as we clung to each other.

Then we heard the gunmen—who we later learned were two boys from our own school—enter the library. They laughed as they shot students at random. I cried and hid my face behind the thick beam that went across the underside of the table. I continued to pray desperately.

Then I felt searing pain as gunfire hit me. The force of it knocked me out from under the table. "God help me!" I screamed, and then looked up, directly at the gunmen.

"Do you believe in God?" one of them demanded.

At first I was terrified to say yes, but then knew I couldn't lie.

"Yes," I said.

"Why?" they asked, taunting.

I mumbled, now in a daze from my wounds, "It's what my parents have taught me. It's what I believe." Then I hid under the table again, weak from blood loss and hoping they would leave me alone. Miraculously, they turned away and eventually left the library.

"Lauren!" I said, nudging my friend who still lay beneath the table. "We can go now. They're gone!" But Lauren didn't move.

"Wake up!" I tried again. "They're gone."

There was no response.

Maybe she's passed out, I thought. Then, peeking over Lauren, I saw students running out an emergency exit.

I was completely covered in blood, and knew that I had been hurt badly. Bunching up the bottom of my shirt, I pressed it against my stomach, trying to stop the bleeding. I had to get out of there! Hoping that someone could come back for Lauren, I mustered all my strength and ran out the door. I made it to a police car parked away from the building. A policeman and students were hiding behind the automobile, and I made it to the grass behind it and collapsed.

Another student, a junior, noticed me there. Though wounded himself, he grabbed a sweatshirt and came over to me.

"Hi," he said. "You're a senior, aren't you? Where are you going to school next year?"

I tried to talk to him, but I cringed when he pushed the sweatshirt against my bleeding abdomen. At that moment, I hated him, not realizing that he was working to help save my life.

"Don't you go to sleep!" the boy commanded.

Finally, I was taken to the hospital, where doctors prodded and poked at me. I was so scared, and wanted my parents, Mark and Shari Schnurr. Finally, they arrived. The doctors told them that I had nine shotgun wounds and numerous shrapnel injuries. They were amazed I was alive. Divine intervention, they said, must have saved my life.

The pain—and the horrible shock of what I had been through—was hard to deal with. But my parents did a good job of comforting me. They protected me from additional horror by keeping all newspapers away and the TV off.

Famous people came to talk to me. Flowers and cards of support poured in from all over the world. It was touching to see how much people cared. But even more comforting was seeing my parents, my two younger sisters, and my good friends—the people who truly care for me.

I slowly began to heal, struggling to keep my faith and deal with the physical injuries. Then, four days after the shooting, I asked my mom and a friend, "How's Lauren?"

They were silent. I could see the answer in their faces, and I started crying. Lauren, smart and high-spirited Lauren, had died in the library.

So much had been lost that day at Columbine. Lauren and twelve other innocent people lost their lives before the two killers shot themselves in the school.

I spent a week in the hospital as I recovered from surgery, but the mental wounds ran much deeper. Questions continually raced through my mind. Why did they do it? Why did innocent people die? Why did Lauren die while I lived?

Now, as I sat at graduation, watching Lauren's family receive the diploma their daughter had earned, I knew there were no answers to these questions. Two of the other girls who were with me in the library that day also were wounded, and I watched them receive their diplomas—and begin a new part of their lives. Eventually it was my turn to receive that hard-earned piece of paper. As my name was called and I took my diploma, I was surprised by the sound of clapping. Looking out, I saw the entire audience standing, sharing my joy of achievement, recovery, and a second chance at life.

I know I lost a lot that day at Columbine, but that was only one day. There are so many other precious memories of high school. Even though it was difficult, I'll always be thankful that I was well enough to attend the last three days of school my senior year. It was my way of taking back what had been stolen from me—my good memories of a great time in life.

My faith in God has been strengthened since that day. I don't know why the shootings happened, but I do believe there is a reason I was spared. Good can overcome evil, and now I focus on what I can do with my life.

Soon I'll begin college to become a teacher and later a guidance counselor. I'm determined to try to help others. I don't want to forget, but instead want to work for change. Maybe someday, I can be that person who reaches out to a student in need. Maybe I can make a difference in somebody else's life.

A Mother's Love

DAVID GIANNELLI
FROM *CHICKEN SOUP FOR THE PET LOVER'S SOUL*

i am a New York City fireman. Being a firefighter has its grim side. When someone's business or home is destroyed, it can break your heart. You see a lot of terror and sometimes even death. But the day I found Scarlett was different. That was a day about life. And love.

It was a Friday. We'd responded to an early morning alarm in Brooklyn at a burning garage. As I was getting my gear on, I heard the sound of cats crying. I couldn't stop—I would have to look for the cats after the fire was put out.

This was a large fire, so there were other hook and ladder companies there as well. We had been told that everyone in the building had made it out safely. I sure hoped so—the entire garage was filled with flames, and it would have been futile for anyone to attempt a rescue anyway. It took a long time and many firefighters to finally bring the enormous blaze under control.

At that point I was free to investigate the cat noises, which I still heard. There continued to be a tremendous amount of smoke and intense

59

heat coming from the building. I couldn't see much, but I followed the meowing to a spot on the sidewalk about five feet away from the front of the garage. There, crying and huddled together, were three terrified little kittens. Then I found two more, one in the street and one across the street. They must have been in the building, as their fur was badly singed. I yelled for a box and out of the crowd around me, one appeared. Putting the five kittens in the box, I carried them to the porch of a neighboring house. I started looking for a mother cat. It was obvious that the mother had gone into the burning garage and carried each of her babies, one by one, out to the sidewalk. Five separate trips into that raging heat and deadly smoke—it was hard to imagine. Then she had attempted to get them across the street, away from the building. Again, one at a time. But she hadn't been able to finish the job. What had happened to her?

A cop told me he had seen a cat go into a vacant lot near where I'd found the last two kittens. She was there, lying down and crying. She was horribly burnt: her eyes were blistered shut, her paws were blackened, and her fur was singed all over her body. In some places you could see her reddened skin showing through the burned fur. She was too weak to move anymore. I went over to her slowly, talking gently as I approached. I figured that she was a wild cat and I didn't want to alarm her. When I picked her up, she cried out in pain, but she didn't struggle. The poor animal reeked of burnt fur and flesh. She gave me a look of utter exhaustion and then relaxed in my arms as much as her pain would allow. Sensing her trust in me, I felt my throat tighten and the tears start in my eyes. I was determined to save this brave little cat and her family. Their lives were, literally, in my hands.

I put the cat in the box with the mewing kittens. Even in her pathetic condition, the blinded mother circled in the box and touched each kitten with her nose, one by one, to make sure they were all there and all safe. She was content, in spite of her pain, now that she was sure the kittens were all accounted for.

These cats obviously needed immediate medical care. I thought of a very special animal shelter out on Long Island, the North Shore Animal League, where I had taken a severely burned dog I had rescued eleven years earlier. If anyone could help them, they could.

I called to alert the Animal League that I was on my way with a badly burned cat and her kittens. Still in my smoke-stained fire gear, I drove my truck there as fast as I could.

When I pulled into the driveway, I saw two teams of vets and technicians standing in the parking lot waiting for me. They whisked the cats into a treatment room—the mother on a table with one vet team and all the kittens on another table with the second team.

Utterly exhausted from fighting the fire, I stood in the treatment room, keeping out of the way. I didn't have much hope that these cats would survive. But somehow, I just couldn't leave them. After a long wait, the vets told me they would observe the kittens and their mother overnight, but they weren't very optimistic about the mother's chances of survival.

I returned the next day and waited and waited. I was about to completely give up hope when the vets finally came over to me. They told me the good news—the kittens would survive.

"And the mother?" I asked. I was afraid to hear the reply. It was still too early to know.

I came back every day, but each day it was the same thing: they just didn't know.

About a week after the fire, I arrived at the shelter in a bleak mood, thinking, *Surely if mother cat was going to make it, she'd have come around by now. How much longer could she hover between life and death?*

But when I walked in the door, the vets greeted me with big smiles and gave me the thumbs up sign! Not only was she going to be all right—in time she'd even be able to see again.

Now that she was going to live, she needed a name. One of the technicians came up with the name Scarlett, because of her reddened skin.

Knowing what Scarlett had endured for her kittens, it melted my heart to see her reunited with them. And what did mama cat do first? Another head count! She touched each of her kittens again, nose to nose, to be sure they were all still safe and sound. She had risked her life, not once, but five times—and it had paid off. All of her babies had survived.

As a firefighter, I see heroism every day. But what Scarlett showed me that day was the height of heroism—the kind of bravery that comes only from a mother's love.

Reach high, for stars lie hidden in your soul.
Dream deep for every dream precedes the goal.

—*Author unknown*

Watch Me, Dad!

ROBERT H. SCHULLER
FROM *POWER IDEAS FOR A HAPPY FAMILY*

Lou Little was football coach at Georgetown University. The college president came to him one day and, naming a student, said, "Lou, do you know this fellow?"

"Sure," Lou answered, "he's been on my squad four years. I've never played him. He's good enough—he's just not motivated."

"Well," the president continued, "we just heard that his father died. Will you break the news to him?"

The coach put his arm around the boy in a back room, "Take a week off, son, I'm sorry." It was Tuesday. Friday, Coach Little came into his locker room to see the student back and suiting up. "What are you doing back already?" Little inquired.

"The funeral was yesterday, coach. So I came back. You see, tomorrow's the big game and I've got to play in it."

"Wait a minute, son," Little said, "you know I've never started you."

"But you will start me tomorrow and you won't be sorry," the moist-eyed boy stated firmly.

Softening, the coach decided that if he won the toss-up he would use the boy on the first play. He couldn't do any damage on the first return. Well, Georgetown won the toss. On the first play this fatherless boy came tearing down the field like a tornado. Coach Little, shocked, left him in for another play. He blocked, he tackled, he passed, he ran. He literally won the ball game that day for Georgetown University.

In the locker room Coach Little, perplexed, asked, "Son, what happened?"

The happy, perspiring victor said, "Coach, you never knew my dad, did you? Well, sir, he was blind and today was the first time he ever saw me play."

Safe Landing

Shoot for the moon.
Even if you miss, you'll land among the stars.

—Les Brown

The Real Winner

AMANDA CORNWALL
AGE 14
FROM *TREASURES 3: STORIES AND ART BY STUDENTS IN JAPAN AND OREGON*

This is crazy," I thought as I bent down to stretch out my cramped, tense leg muscles. There I was, a mere freshman in the middle of my first year of competitive swimming, about to swim the dreaded 500—twenty grueling lengths across the seemingly endless pool. Me! The one who's always picked last for every sport in PE, the one who whispers her disgraceful physical aptitude score to the teacher instead of proudly announcing it out loud! At the beginning of the season, my coach called me (affectionately, I think) "The Drowner," making private bets with the assistant coach about how long I would last on the team. They were sure I would quit after the first two days. Despite their incredible faith in me, I stuck with it. And now, there I was, about to swim the hardest race I would ever encounter!

I hadn't a prayer of winning. How did I get myself into this, anyway? Oh yeah, one of the seniors scheduled for the race hurt her shoulder. So, the assistant coach smirked when he asked me, "Wanna swim the five hundred?" I must have had a temporary failure of my otherwise fair mental capacities: I said yes. Perhaps I wanted to prove that in spite of my skinny body I wasn't a frail wimp. Perhaps it was simply because I wanted to see the look on the assistant coach's face when I accepted.

"I just did, that's all!" I muttered aloud as I straightened my goggles. The girl next to me raised an eyebrow, I blushed. Suddenly, the irritating man with the microphone called out the words I feared: "Girls' five hundred freestyle. Swimmers up!"

"This is it!" I mumbled to the clear blue water beneath me as I stepped up to the starting block.

"Take your marks," he demanded.

"*Good-bye world!*" I thought as I bent down to curl my fingers and toes around the metal edge of the block. A muted silence of tense anticipation settled throughout the pool. As I waited for the start off sound, my senses turned inward to focus on the steady crescendo of my heartbeat. Bleeeeeeep! The blaring signal shattered the fragile stillness. Instantly I reacted, shoving off the block with all my might. Still, my dive was a foot short of the other swimmers' dives.

The sudden shock of the icy water was electrifying. I broke the surface and began to swim, my confidence growing with each new stroke. My only thoughts were "stroke-two-three-four, breathe-stroke-two-three-four... ." as my body took control. Relaxing, I found my rhythm.

For the first lap and a half, everyone sprinted and we stayed relatively close together. But too soon, the faster swimmers began to pull away, and I was left behind. From then on, I took no notice of the other swimmers. I saw only the walls in front of me and the cruel counter card telling me that I had swum only nine lengths. It felt like a thousand. Don't worry. Keep going, you can do it! I told myself with all the enthusiasm I could muster. I got my second wind after that, as though my batteries had been recharged. There was more power in my strokes and my kicks were stronger. I gave myself a brief reassuring comment at each turn.

By the thirteenth length I felt great—almost too great. I'm so proud of you! I told myself. I felt invincible, as though I could do anything I wanted. I felt like swimming the English Channel. No, make that the Atlantic!

Then, all of the sudden, I felt like I absolutely could never swim another stroke as long as I lived! Pain and panic replaced my fantasy world. My legs ached, my lungs burned, and my rhythm fell apart. My only thoughts were to vacate this pool and never come back. Give it up! I told myself, struggling through chilly water that felt as thick as swamp mud. Just think how wonderful it would feel to climb out and take a long, hot shower.

"No!" I pushed the weak thought out of my mind. I thought instead of the dreadful humiliation giving up would bring. You're not a quitter! Determination formed a wall of steel in my mind. I would finish this race if it killed me.

Again I found my rhythm and forced my body to swim. The pistol sounded at my fifteenth length, warning the rest of the swimmers that the leader was on her final two. I stopped thinking and painfully swam on. Eventually, the card showed no more numbers, only the blessed neon orange rectangles that meant I was on my final lap. I performed my last flip turn and began my home stretch. When the wall appeared before me for the last time, it felt like an angel of mercy had swooped down to embrace me. I punched the touch-pad with my last drop of strength.

I managed to stagger over to the cold metal bench where my towel lay. Scooping it up, I gave a few half-hearted attempts at drying myself off then collapsed in a heap on the bench. As I lay there panting, the pain and exhaustion were gradually replaced by feelings of pride, accomplishment, and glory. I heard my coach congratulating the swimmer who had touched the wall first.

No, I thought to myself. Coach, you're congratulating the wrong person. Her race will come later, at the state meet and beyond, where she will dazzle all observers with her strength and talent. This was my race, and I won it. My victory was different. I had triumphed over my own insecurity, my own pain, my own weakness, and everyone else's doubts.

ᴀ Big Old Grin

ANN TAIT
AGE 14
FROM *WHERE THE HEART IS*

Sometimes the lessons that you learn in life come from the people you least expect them from. My little brother, Jimmy, is twelve years old. He's also mentally and physically handicapped. He had a stroke before he was born, and parts of his body (his toes and his brain) didn't completely form.

But even though those things aren't completely what they should be, I think Jimmy made up for it in the area of his heart. When we go out in public, there are people who stare at us, who won't even come near us, because they're afraid—afraid of my baby brother.

I've seen kids as little as four stick out their tongues and make evil little faces at him as though he weren't even human. But Jimmy never gets angry. He doesn't beat them up or hate them forever. He just gives them a big old grin.

It's amazing to watch. First, his big, brown eyes grow sparkly, and the corners of his mouth begin to twitch. Then, when his smile does break, and his small, white teeth peek through those lips, it's as if the sun has broken through the clouds.

Some people say they feel sorry for Jimmy and that it's too bad he isn't "normal." But you know what? In a way, I wish everyone on this earth was like my brother. Because no matter how mean people are to him, he always has a smile.

So now, if people are mean to me or make fun of me, I just give them a big old grin, because I've learned from my little brother that it's not how much your brain has developed, or how many toes you have, it's how much your heart feels and how big a smile you wear.

Treasure

Each day is a treasure box of gifts from God,
just waiting to be opened.
Open your gifts with excitement.
You will find forgiveness attached to ribbons of joy.
You will find love wrapped in sparkling gems.

—Joan Clayton

Unbelievable!

NORMAN VINCENT PEALE
FROM *YOU CAN IF YOU THINK YOU CAN*

In 1970, Tom Dempsey kicked that unbelievable sixty-three-yard field goal that electrified the athletic world.

Tom was born with only half a right foot and a deformed right hand. He had some really great parents, for never once did they make him uncomfortably aware of his handicap. As a result the boy did everything everybody else did. If the Scouts hiked ten miles, so did Tom. Why not? There was nothing wrong with him. He could do it, same as any other kid.

Then he wanted to play football and, of all things, he got the desire to excel in a special talent. He found he could kick a football farther than anybody with whom he played. To capitalize on that ability he had a special shoe designed. With never a negative thought about the half right foot and deformed right hand, he showed up at a kicking tryout camp and was given a contract with the Chargers.

The coach, as gently as he could say it, gave him the word that he "didn't have what it takes to make it in pro football." And urged him to try something else. Finally he applied to the New Orleans Saints and begged for a chance. The coach was doubtful, but was impressed by the boy's belief in himself, so took him on.

Two weeks later the coach was even more impressed when Tom Dempsey kicked a fifty-five-yard field goal in an exhibition game. That got him the job of regular kicker for the Saints, and in that season he scored ninety-nine points for his team. Then came the big moment. The stadium was packed with sixty-six thousand fans. The ball was on the twenty-eight-yard line, with only a few seconds left to play. The play advanced the ball to the forty-five-yard line. Now there was time for only one play. "Go in there and kick it, Dempsey," the coach shouted.

As Tom ran onto the field he knew his team was fifty-five yards from the goal line, or sixty-three yards from the point at which he would have to kick. The longest kick ever in a regular game had been fifty-five yards by Bert Rechichar of the Baltimore Colts.

The snap of the ball was perfect. Dempsey put his foot into the ball squarely. It went straight, but would it be far enough? The sixty-six thousand spectators watched breathlessly. The official in the end zone raised his hands, signaling it was good. The ball had cleared the bar by inches. The team won, 19–17. The stands went wild, thrilled by the longest field goal ever kicked. And by a player with half a foot and a deformed hand!

"Unbelievable!" someone shouted. But Dempsey smiled. He remembered his parents. They had always told him what he could do, not what he couldn't do. He accomplished this tremendous feat because, as he so well put it, "They never told me I couldn't."

Twelve Five-Dollar Bills

JEFF LEELAND
WITH TRACY SUMNER
ADAPTED FROM *ONE SMALL SPARROW*

Thirteen-year-old Dameon Sharkey had his own adversities to endure, his own physical problems to overcome, his own challenges to meet. Dameon stood out in a crowd. He didn't dress like most junior high school students, wearing big black stretch pants, a white button-down shirt, and a tie to school every day.

A teenager who had few friends and who struggled in school, Dameon didn't seem like the kind of boy who would ever make much of a difference in the world around him. All the same, Dameon became a hero in his community and, in particular, to one family facing some adversity of its own.

Jeff Leeland, Dameon's teacher in his adaptive physical education class, and his wife, Kristi, had just received a devastating piece of news: Their six-month-old son Michael, their fourth child, had been diagnosed with a pre-leukemia condition that would require him to undergo a bone marrow transplant in order to save his life.

Worse yet, because Jeff had been at his job for only a short time, the

Leelands' insurance company refused to cover the $175,000 bill just to get little Michael admitted to the hospital for the operation. Doctors had told the Leelands that their six-year-old daughter Amy's bone marrow was a perfect match for Michael's. With that hill climbed, the Leeland family faced what looked like an impossible mountain.

Time was running short for Michael. Unless he had the marrow transplant soon, there was little chance he would live long.

It seemed like a hopeless situation. Jeff Leeland's little boy was dying, and there was nothing he could do about it. He felt defeated and wounded by what was happening in his and his family's lives. All he could do was pray. In the midst of his prayer, the calming assurance came over him that God was in control.

Jeff Leeland had become one of Dameon's favorite teachers, and the young man couldn't stand by and do nothing when he saw his teacher's need. Dameon went to his bank, withdrew his life savings—$60 cash—then limped into Jeff Leeland's office to make his donation.

"Mr. Leeland," the concerned young man told his teacher. "You're my partner. If your baby's in trouble, I want to help out." Dameon then held out his hand and handed the stunned teacher twelve $5 bills. After gratefully hugging Dameon and thanking him for his generosity, Jeff Leeland went to the principal's office, and they agreed to use Dameon's gift to start the "Michael Leeland Fund."

Soon, Dameon's classmates began following his example, starting their personal drive to raise money for Michael's operation. They wrote letters, made phone calls, held raffles, set up donation boxes, and contacted local media about the story. One ninth-grader named Jon went out in his spare time and knocked on doors in his neighborhood to ask for donations. The cause of Michael Leeland became more than a fundraiser for the students at Kamiakin Junior High School. It became these young people's "mission of mercy."

Soon after Dameon's original gift, the donations quickly started flowing in. The foundation received donations as small as $1 and as large as $10,000. One man who was $35,000 in debt and had just lost his job sent $10, and a prison inmate sent $25. One little second-grader brought in a bag of pennies from her piggy bank, and a local eighth-grader named "Mary" cashed in $300 in savings bonds and donated the money to the fund.

Before long, the flow of generosity became a flood, and within a week of the original gift, the fund had grown to more than $16,000. The torrent of gifts continued for the following weeks, and less than a month after it was started, the Michael Leeland Fund had ballooned to an astonishing $220,000. More than enough to cover the cost of Michael's medical bills.

That summer, Michael endured twelve days of chemotherapy and radiation treatment before undergoing the operation to transplant his sister's bone marrow into his body. It was an ordeal for Michael and his family, but on his first birthday they received the news that his white cell count had surpassed the minimum level. Four years later, Michael's cancer was in remission, his body healthy enough to allow him to start playing T-ball for one of the local teams. He talks often of wanting to excel as an athlete, and, thanks to the generosity of Dameon Sharkey and the efforts of his classmates, he will have the opportunity to do so.

Not only did the Michael Leeland Fund grow large enough to enable Michael to receive life-saving medical treatment, it grew to a fund now known as the Sparrow Foundation, a nonprofit organization that helps young people in schools, churches, and youth organizations to reach out to their young neighbors who are in medical need.

And it was the generosity and compassion of one concerned, softhearted teenager that got it started. Dameon Sharkey didn't have much to give, but what he had he gave gladly.

As it turns out, it was more than enough.

Theodore Geisel

DAN OWEN
FROM *CHRISTIAN YOUTH NEWS*

L̲ike lots of kids, young Theodore Geisel used to sit in school and doodle strange little drawings. He took an art class in high school. The teacher told Theodore not to plan to make a living from drawing. "You're never going to make it."

After high school, Theodore went to Dartmouth College, the prestigious Ivy League school, and took a class on writing because he thought maybe he could be a writer. Again he heard a teacher encourage him to find another calling. "You don't quite have what it takes."

Theodore's fraternity voted him least likely to succeed. No matter. He kept drawing the strange characters and writing funny stories. He sent them to twenty-seven publishers, and twenty-seven publishers turned him down, saying there was no market.

The twenty-eighth publisher proved them all wrong, and Dr. Seuss was born. Theodore Geisel, the doodling student without a future in art and writing, wrote forty-eight books translated into twenty languages that sold over two hundred million copies.

75

Lots of people called Theodore Geisel a failure. At times he must have thought he was. But someone saw something that other people didn't see, and he became a success.

Do not follow where the path may lead.
Go instead where there is no path, and leave a trail.

—*Author unknown*

The King's Great Gift

AUTHOR UNKNOWN

There once was a wise and beloved king who cared greatly for his people and wanted only what was the best for them. The people knew the king took personal interest in their affairs and tried to understand how his decisions affected their lives. Periodically, he would disguise himself and wander through the streets, trying to see life from their perspective.

One day he disguised himself as a poor villager and went to visit the public baths. Many people were there enjoying the fellowship and relaxation. The water for the baths was heated by a furnace in the cellar, where one man was responsible for maintaining the comfort level of the water. The king made his way to the basement to visit with the man who tirelessly tended the fire.

The two men shared a meal together, and the king befriended this lonely man. Day after day, week in and week out, the king went to visit the firetender. The man in the cellar soon became close to his strange visitor because he came down to the basement where he was. No one else ever had showed that much caring or concern.

One day the king revealed his true identity to his friend. It was a risky move, for he feared that the man might ask him for special favors or a gift. Instead, the king's new friend looked into his eyes and said, "You left your comfortable palace to sit with me in this hot and dingy cellar. You ate my meager food and genuinely showed you cared about what happens to me. On other people you might bestow rich gifts, but to me you have given the greatest gift of all. You gave me the gift of yourself."

The Blind Bomber

BRUCE NASH AND ALLAN ZULLO
FROM *THE GREATEST SPORTS STORIES NEVER TOLD*

The eyes of college basketball player George Glamack were so bad that he couldn't see the rim of the basket. To him, the backboard was only a dim blur.

Yet, incredibly, Glamack became one of the top scorers in the history of the University of North Carolina. He also earned All-America and the school's College Player of the Year honors in 1940 and 1941.

Because of his poor eyesight and his amazingly accurate hook shots, George was dubbed "The Blind Bomber," a nickname he wore proudly.

In fact, the worse Glamack saw, the better he shot!

As a child, George suffered from poor eyesight, but he refused to tell anyone. He didn't want to wear glasses out of fear that kids would tease him. Despite his vision problems, George turned into a fine young athlete. But at the age of fourteen, Glamack was half-blinded from a football injury.

It happened during a sandlot game in his hometown of Allentown, Pennsylvania. George was stiff-armed when he tried to tackle a ball carrier and was accidentally poked in the left eye. At first, doctors thought he would be blind in that eye for life. But George's mother spent weeks attending to her injured son, changing the dressing on his damaged eye several times a day. His mom's tender loving care saved Glamack's eye, but he never fully recovered his sight. Combined with the poor vision in his other eye, George could not see clearly past a few feet.

Yet the husky, athletic teenager was determined to continue playing all sports.

Basketball was his first love. But when Glamack tried playing again after his eye healed, he couldn't see the basket and could barely make out the backboard. He lost confidence in his ability to shoot, and instead of becoming a starter on the high school team, he wound up on the bench.

George prayed every night for help in regaining his confidence. One day during a high school game, Glamack was sent in for mop-up duty in the last minute. A teammate passed the ball to George. On a lark, George tried a hook shot from fifteen feet away even though he couldn't see the basket. Incredibly, his blind shot swished through the hoop! To George, his prayers had been answered. He knew then and there that despite his poor eyesight, he would one day be a basketball star.

So he developed his own "Braille" system. He knew that the foul line, the lane, and other markings painted on the court were a fixed distance from the basket. Using the markings as guides, Glamack knew exactly where to shoot without ever looking at the basket. Since he didn't need to see the hoop, George spent hundreds of hours perfecting a shot that was almost impossible to guard against. He would turn his back to the basket and shoot deadly hook shots with either hand. From then on, he was a dazzling shooter in high school. When he graduated, George had grown to six feet, six inches and weighed two hundred pounds and was recruited by the Tar Heels of North Carolina. He turned into a high-scoring starter by his junior year with the help of teammate Bob Rose, a forward with exceptional passing abilities. The two used whistles to communicate. Whenever George heard a certain whistle, he would get in position at a certain spot on the court and wait for a pass from Rose. True to form, the Blind Bomber would turn his back to the basket and score with one of his sweeping hook shots. Because Glamack was so much taller than most players in those days, defenders were seldom able to stop his high-arching hook shots.

In his junior year, George averaged twenty points a game as the Tar Heels soared to a lofty 23–3 record, their best ever at the time. They placed second in the Southern Conference, but won the conference tournament championship. At the end of the season, Glamack collected his first unanimous All America award and was named the Helms Foundation's College Player of the Year.

The following season, the Blind Bomber resumed his blistering scoring pace. Against Clemson, the Bomber poured in forty-five points to set a new conference mark and was on his way to breaking the then national single-game record of fifty points when he fouled out with three and one half minutes left to play.

Later, in losing to Dartmouth 60–59 in the consolation game of the NCAA finals, Glamack scored thirty-one points, a single-game tournament record that stood for eleven years. In his final season as a collegiate player, Glamack again made every All-America team and repeated as Player of the Year.

Glamack's sensational shooting did more than help put North Carolina basketball on the map. He inspired millions of young people to overcome hardships and disabilities in order to reach their goals.

When his playing days were over, Glamack's number was retired, one of the few given that honor. Today, hanging in North Carolina's Smith Center Arena, his number twenty has been an inspiration to other great Tar Heel hoops stars such as Michael Jordan, James Worthy, and Bobby Jones.

For My Sister

DAVID C. NEEDHAM
FROM *CLOSE TO HIS MAJESTY*

There is a true story of a little boy whose sister needed a blood transfusion. The doctor explained that she had the same disease the boy had recovered from two years earlier. Her only chance of recovery was a transfusion from someone who had previously conquered the disease. Since the two children had the same rare blood type, the boy was an ideal donor.

"Would you give your blood to Mary?" the doctor asked.

Johnny hesitated. His lower lip started to tremble. Then he smiled and said, "Sure, for my sister."

Soon the two children were wheeled into the hospital room. Mary, pale and thin. Johnny, robust and healthy. Neither spoke, but when their eyes met, Johnny grinned.

As the nurse inserted the needle into his arm, Johnny's smile faded. He watched the blood flow through the tube.

With the ordeal almost over, Johnny's voice, slightly shaky, broke the silence.

"Doctor, *when do I die?*"

Only then did the doctor realize why Johnny had hesitated, why his lip had trembled when he agreed to donate his blood. He thought giving his blood to his sister would mean giving up his life. In that brief moment, he had made his great decision.

Maria's New Shoes

MARY-PAT HOFFMAN

ur City newspaper carried a story about a young girl from Bosnia-Herzegovina who lost both of her legs in the war. She and her father were struck by the same mortar shell while helping to distribute food from the United States to their countrymen. Her father had died in front of her. It was impossible to try to imagine all that she had been through.

I remember looking at the news photographs over and over again during the course of the day. I'd put the paper down only to find myself returning for another look an hour later.

By that evening, I decided to write Maria an upbeat note. I told her about happy times I've enjoyed on horseback, at dances, while attending college, bicycling with my daughter on the beach, and in my career and married life. I also mentioned that I, too, had been fourteen years old when I began to use an artificial leg.

Before sealing the envelope, I added that I would be happy to send Maria a gift of new shoes. I pledged to take my daughter along to ensure the shoes would be "cool" and said how much having great shoes had meant to me during similar days.

I felt good about making the offer, but felt sure that I would never hear back. I couldn't have been more wrong. Two days later I received a call from the prosthetics firm where Maria was a patient telling me that my card had already be selected and read to Maria through an interpreter. When I voiced my surprise, the woman said my letter was "the best one" Maria had received.

She then explained that they were going to have a national press conference for Maria the following Tuesday, and asked if I could send a pair of shoes that weekend. We launched into a discussion about the color of the outfit Maria would be wearing. She then suggested that I fly up to meet Maria and be a part of the occasion. I assured her that Maria would have her shoes in time for the press conference, but I would need time to think about making the journey.

My daughter and I traipsed from store to store the next day in mad pursuit of exactly the right pair of hot pink tennis shoes. We ended up buying two pairs of shoes, hair ornaments, an assortment of socks, and a purse before dashing off to mail our gifts to a young girl we'd never met.

By that time I knew that I would make the trip to meet Maria. When I arrived at the prosthetics center I was amazed by the number of press and media professionals there. It reminded me of a press conference I'd attended for Nancy Reagan several years before. Television and cable crews, radio people, writers, and photographers jammed the room. I could tell that many of them had covered national and international events for many years.

As Maria was wheeled into the room in a wheelchair, I looked into her face and felt as though I knew her. Moments passed before I could bring myself to look down at the hot pink tennis shoes we had selected so carefully. I felt humbled at the sight of them. They were such a small part of what she faced each day.

Word passed through the crowd that her mother and sisters had not seen her wear or walk on artificial legs. And that, until recently, they really didn't understand what artificial legs were all about. I saw the family sitting across the room. Maria answered questions through an interpreter. I stood out of camera range, yet directly in front of her. When she looked at me I did my best to give her a small smile, and the smallest of smiles began to cross her face. Her eyes sought me out again and again. I felt a powerful connection. Then they wheeled her into position in front of the walking rails. Her strength and determination were palpable. I found myself thinking that she is exactly the human being she needs to be to live out her destiny.

Memories flooded my mind and tears came into my eyes as I watched her reach out her arms to take hold of the rails. I understood that moment. As she pulled herself up, there was an audible gasp and sounds of quiet crying from the area of the room her family occupied. And then she began to walk. Slowly at first, with spotters on either side, but with colt-like grace. She was amazing.

Newsmen and women throughout the room were quietly shedding tears—even the men I had pegged as seasoned veterans of nearly everything were forced to lower their cameras and wipe away tears before going back to the work at hand.

Pretty young Maria finished her exercises standing alone, without support, with her arms raised above her head. A remarkable achievement for any one who has only been "up on their legs" for a matter of hours.

After the ceremony, I was introduced to her as the woman who sent the shoes. "Thank you very much," she said, in almost perfect English. We talked through the interpreter about how to wear miniskirts and high heels with prosthetic devices. Our visit ended with hugs and kisses.

Maria's mother and I hugged wordlessly for a minute. There wasn't a sound in the room. As we ended our embrace, I tried to conjure up a way to tell her that Maria would be all right. Was all right. Is all right. I tried saying in a voice much to loud that Maria was "OK." No response. "She's fine!" Again no response. Finally, I gave her the "thumbs-up" hand signal. As a look of understanding crossed her face, we both broke into broad grins and the kind of laughter that defies differences of language, continents, and even war.

She knew then that Maria would be all right. And I understood how much Maria helped me connect once again with the frightened fourteen-year-old I had been so long ago and appreciate her courage—perhaps for the very first time.

More Out of Life

JOE WHITE
FROM *OVER THE EDGE AND BACK*

Wes, as the boy's friends know him, had what John Wayne called grit. General Patton called it guts. Vince Lombardi called it "the stuff it takes to be a winner." The Bible calls it endurance. Wesley White certainly has 'em all. His life story would make a box office smash hit in a Hollywood movie or a best-selling novel at the bookstore. This story is true.

At age one-and-a-half, a Texas doctor discovered diabetes in Wesley's chemistry imbalance. Taking insulin shots daily for the rest of his life isn't something an eighteen-month-old wants to dream about. But the insulin seizures that were to come were worse than the needle.

As if that weren't enough for one person to bear, when Wes was two-and-a-half, another doctor diagnosed a greater complication: Wesley was epileptic. The two disorders immediately began to trigger each other. During a six-month period of intense hospitalization, Wesley would have seizures (grand mal—the worst kind, with falls and head bruises) as often as one every minute. He wore a hockey helmet in the hospital to protect himself. The doctors told his parents that Wes would never grow up, that he would always be confined, and that there was probably permanent brain damage.

The doctors couldn't have been further from the truth. The problem was that they didn't measure the size of Wesley's heart. That heart began to drive Wesley to becoming not just "normal," but extraordinary.

In sixth grade he took up boxing for a sport. Wes looks back at the next three years in the ring and smiles: "It was a challenge. I liked to go into the ring alone and have to stand up for a few minutes while another guy tried to take me off my feet. I never wanted to destroy the opponent, I just wanted to win." Win is what Wesley often did. He fought his way to the state championships, where he was first runner-up.

Now that Wes is in high school, football is his sport. Never mind the diabetes and epilepsy (still a nagging problem). Wes is only five-foot-five and he weighs 120 pounds. Guess what position he plays? You guessed wrong. Defensive tackle! This year he started on the junior varsity as a sophomore. Facing a 200-pound opponent was not unusual. Wesley has gotten used to big obstacles.

Want to know more? Wes has been a rodeo clown. With his father he would do a funny act in the arena in front of a 2000-pound Brahma bull who wasn't in on the joke. "I love to see people laugh and have fun," Wes says.

The medical problems continue. When asked why he doesn't lose heart, Wes says humbly, "I just go on. I don't like to sit. You can have fun if you want to. This disease is mine, and I might as well enjoy it and get the best from life."

This summer he enjoyed life in a kayak on one of America's swiftest and roughest whitewater rivers. Who knows what he'll think of next?

"I believe God loves me," Wes concluded. "He is faithful. He's coming back for me. He's my best friend."

I can see why Wesley White is a winner. Pound for pound, given what he's been given, Wes gets more out of life that any young man I know.

ᴀ Christmas Gift I'll Never Forget

LINDA DEMERS HUMMEL
FROM *FAMILY CIRCLE* MAGAZINE

He entered my life twenty years ago, leaning against the doorjamb of Room 202, where I taught fifth grade. He wore sneakers three sizes too large and checkered pants ripped at the knees.

Daniel, as I'll call him, though that was not his real name, made this undistinguished entrance in the school of a quaint lakeside village known for its old money, white colonial homes, and brass mailboxes. He told me his last school had been in a neighboring county. "We were pickin' fruit," he said matter-of-factly.

I suspected this friendly, scruffy, smiling boy from a migrant family had no idea he had been thrown into a den of fifth-grade lions who had never before seen torn pants. If he noticed snickering, he didn't let on. There was no chip on his shoulder.

Twenty-five children eyed Daniel suspiciously until the kickball game that afternoon. Then he led off the first inning with a home run. With it came a bit of respect from the wardrobe critics of Room 202.

Next was Charles's turn. Charles was the least athletic, most overweight child in the history of fifth grade. After his second strike, amid the rolled eyes and groans of the class, Daniel edged up and spoke quietly to Charles's dejected back. "Forget them, kid. You can do it."

Charles warmed, smiled, stood taller and promptly struck out anyway. But at that precise moment, defying the social order of this jungle he had entered, Daniel had gently begun to change things—and us.

By autumn's end, we had all gravitated toward him. He taught us all kinds of lessons. How to call a wild turkey. How to tell whether fruit is ripe before that first bite. How to treat others, even Charles. Especially Charles. He never did use our names, calling me "Miss" and the students "kid."

The day before Christmas vacation, the students always brought gifts for the teacher. It was a ritual—opening each department-store box, surveying the expensive perfume or scarf or leather wallet, and thanking the child.

That afternoon, Daniel walked to my desk and bent close to my ear. "Our packing boxes came out last night," he said without emotion. "We're leavin' tomorrow."

As I grasped the news, my eyes filled with tears. He countered the awkward silence by telling me about the move. Then, as I regained my composure, he pulled a gray rock from his pocket. Deliberately and with great style, he pushed it gently across my desk.

I sensed that this was something remarkable, but all my practice with perfume and silk had left me pitifully unprepared to respond. "It's for you," he said, fixing his eyes on mine. "I polished it up special."

I've never forgotten that moment.

Years have passed since then. Each Christmas my daughter asks me to tell this story. It always begins after she has picked up the small polished rock that sits on my desk and nestles herself in my lap. The first words of the story never vary. "The last time I ever saw Daniel, he gave me this rock as a gift and told me about his boxes. That was a long time ago, even before you were born.

"He's a grown-up now," I finish. Together we wonder where he is and what he has become.

"Someone good I bet," my daughter says. Then she adds, "Do the end of the story."

I know what she wants to hear—the lesson of love and caring learned by a teacher from a boy with nothing—and everything—to give. A boy who lived out of boxes. I touch the rock, remembering.

"Hi kid," I say softly. "This is Miss. I hope you no longer need the packing boxes. And Merry Christmas, wherever you are."

Friends

Things I've Learned Lately...

Summer is my favorite season,
Friends don't always have to get along,
There's so much more inside people we don't see,
And everyone looks for love.

Sunshine

SARAH WOOD
FROM FRIENDS

The silence was almost unbearably uncomfortable. I was too nervous to speak, and I think everyone else was too. The car ride seemed endless. Once in a while we would look at each other and force a smile, but our smiles were more nervous than warm.

I don't know what she was thinking about, but I know that memories flooded my head. I was remembering my first day of school when I felt like there was a spotlight shining on me and someone had written "new" on my forehead. She simply looked at me, took my hand, and said, "Come on. I'll help you find your homeroom."

Then there was the time I missed the winning foul shot in a sixth-grade basketball game. The other team was up by one point, and I got fouled just as the buzzer went off. I was allowed one-and-one foul shots, but I missed the first one and the other team won the game. I was angry at myself and apologetic to my team. I felt as though I had let the whole world down. I sat on the bleachers with my head in my hands. Suddenly

I felt her hand rest on my shoulder and a flood of warmth and understanding run through me. When I looked up, she saw how crushed I was and tears came to her eyes. She hugged me and told me the story of when she knocked herself out with her own hockey stick during a game. Laughter quickly overcame my tears.

She was also right there when my first boyfriend broke up with me. As I hung up the phone, I could feel tears suffocating my throat. I felt as though someone had taken my heart away from me in a matter of minutes. But once I was enclosed in her arms, I clung to her as though she were the only thing I had left in the world.

As I came back from my daydreams, I realized that our road trip was almost at its end. Only one hour left. She started twirling her hair like she does when she gets nervous. From the backseat where I was sitting I saw a single tear roll down her face. It seemed that it took the rest of the car ride for it to reach her chin.

When we drove onto the enormous campus, the rainstorm that had mysteriously appeared was subsiding. We found our way to her assigned dorm, unpacked her things, and were standing at the car about to say our good-byes. I couldn't do it. I couldn't say good-bye. We stared at each other, tears streaming down our faces. One long hug and a kiss on the cheek were our farewell. I climbed into the car and strapped on my seat belt.

She sat down in the grass and watched us pull out of the driveway. I stared through the rearview mirror at my best friend whom I was leaving behind at college. I stared until the car turned the corner and buildings blocked my view of my sister. I looked up into the sky, and through the leftover clouds I saw one single bright ray of sunshine. It was going to be okay.

Annie

SAMANTHA ECKER
FROM *FRIENDS*

When I was ten years old, I had a lot of friends. But looking back now, my best friend was someone I never really thought of as my friend. I only considered Annie my next-door neighbor.

I didn't know too much about Annie. She was four years older than I was. She went to an art school in the city. Every afternoon as I played in the front yard with my little brother Kevin, I would see Annie walking home from the train station. I remember admiring how mature she looked carrying her big black portfolio as her pretty blond hair blew in the wind. I'd see her bright, friendly smile, and I'd run up to her to say hello. I admired the freckles that graced her face. Annie was the only person I knew who had freckles. I wished that I had freckles and that I was old enough to go to school with her.

Sometimes on weekends, Annie would make up games for Kevin and me to play. We'd go on treasure hunts and put on plays about stories that Annie told to us. Her stories kept us fascinated for hours. I admired a lot of things about Annie, but what I admired most was her imagination.

When Kevin and I would get into trouble and be sent to our rooms, we would look across the driveway to Annie's house. We'd look in the window to see if she was there. If she was, we had a Morse code system devised by Annie to send secret messages to each other.

Once Annie showed us the mural she painted on her bedroom wall. In every color you could imagine, she had painted an assortment of cartoon characters. In my mind, Michelangelo could not have done a more impressive job.

During the summer there was always something to do, thanks to Annie. She would teach us art techniques and show us how to make stone people. She'd make up intricate plots with interesting characters for us to portray. By September, Kevin and I had been spies, detectives, and a myriad of other characters.

One day I was sitting outside on the porch. It was my birthday, but I was sad. I can't remember why. Annie appeared out of nowhere and presented me with a birthday card and a drawing she had done of me. To this day, I still don't know how Annie remembered my birthday, but I'm glad she did.

Now I'm seventeen. Annie is twenty-one. I only see her warm, friendly smile once in a while, but it's the same smile she used to flash at me seven years ago. I'm in high school now, and when I get home from the train station, I see Alex, the little boy who lives down the street, watching me. When I smile at him, he runs up and asks me if I want to play. Sometimes I make up games for Alex and his sister Jenny. Sometimes I think of treasure hunts for them to go on. I teach them the art techniques that Annie taught me. I watch Alex and Jenny laugh as they play with their stone people. It reminds me of when I was ten and when one of the most important people in my life was someone who I never even realized was my best friend.

The Green-Eyed Monster

Teresa Cleary
FROM *WWJD Stories for Teens*

The minute my friend Jenny and I got to the mall, I knew I shouldn't have come with her on this shopping expedition.

"My mom said she thought I'd have more fun shopping with you for my birthday present, so she gave me her credit card and told me to 'be reasonable,'" Jenny said as we entered the clothing store.

I tried to smile at Jenny's remark, but I could tell my effort left something to be desired. I could feel my facial muscles tightening with forced cheerfulness as I imagined what "reasonable" meant. You'll probably only buy three new outfits instead of five I thought, and each one complete with shoes and accessories.

Before I could stop it, the green-eyed monster was rearing its ugly head.

Jenny and I had been best friends since the sixth grade. Over the years, we'd done everything together—gotten our hair cut short and hated it, discovered guys, and complained about school.

At first it never bothered me that Jenny's family was much better off than mine. Now that we were in high school, though, I began noticing the things Jenny had that I didn't—a bulging wardrobe, her own car, membership in a fitness club. It seemed the list could go on forever. More and more I was envious of her lifestyle and the things she had.

I couldn't help comparing this shopping extravaganza with birthdays in my family. Even though we weren't poor, four children in the family meant budgeting even for birthdays. We had a good time, but my parents put a $20 spending limit on presents.

I remembered my last birthday. In our family, it's a tradition that the one who's celebrating a birthday gets to pick the menu and invite one special person to the celebration. I invited Jenny, of course; and ordered my favorite meal complete with chocolate cake for dessert. It was fun, but nothing like this credit card shopping spree.

I was brought back to the present when Jenny held up a white sweater and matching skirt.

"Do you like this?" she asked.

"It is gorgeous," I said. Jenny nodded and continued looking while I moved from rack to rack, touching the beautiful clothes. "I'm going to try this on," Jenny headed for the dressing room. After a few minutes, she reappeared in the outfit she'd just shown me. She looked beautiful.

I sighed. While part of me wanted to tell her how good she looked, another part of me snatched the words back before they were uttered. Jenny was in such good shape that she'd look good in a potato sack. Sometimes I doubted my judgment in choosing a best friend who was so pretty. *Lord, why can't I be the one with the rich parents and the great looks?*

"Well, Teresa, what do you think?"—a question Jenny had asked me more than once. "Do you like it?"

The outfit looked great on her, but the green-eyed monster struck again. "Not really," I lied. "I think you need something with more color."

"You think so?" Jenny said doubtfully. "I don't know."

"Just trust me. We'll find something better," I told her, pushing her back into the dressing room. "You just can't buy the first thing you see." I would have said anything to get Jenny out of the store and away from that outfit. As we left, Jenny gave the sweater one last look.

Just down the mall, we passed a frozen yogurt place. "My treat," Jenny said, pulling out her wallet. "The Taylors stayed out late Saturday night, so I've got a few dollars to spare."

I never could resist chocolate yogurt so we got our cones and sat down at a table. As Jenny chattered away about a million things, I thought about the feelings I'd had toward my best friend lately. Those feelings weren't very kind.

As I sat there, I began to see Jenny in a new light. I saw how attractive Jenny was—not just treating me to yogurt, but in all areas of her life. Even though she was the one who belonged to the fitness club, she took me every chance she got. She also let me drive her car and borrow her clothes.

I also realized this wouldn't be a shopping extravaganza: Jenny would go home with only one gift. I'd let envy take over my vision until it distorted the picture I had of my best friend.

With that thought, the green-eyed monster seemed to shrink in size.

After we finished our cones, we headed for the next clothing store. "Look at that red sweater," Jenny said as we passed the window. "It would be perfect for you, Teresa, with your dark hair. How are you doing saving your baby-sitting money? Maybe you'll have enough soon to buy something like that?"

A few minutes ago, all I would have heard was the part about saving my baby-sitting money. I would have resented the fact that all Jenny had to do was ask her parents for the sweater and they'd buy it for her. This time, though, I heard more. I heard my best friend complimenting me and saying how good I'd look. I heard the voice of someone who loved and cared for me for who I was. I needed to extend that same courtesy to her.

"You know, Jen, I've been thinking," I said, linking my arm with her and pulling her back to the first store, "that white skirt and sweater really was beautiful on you...."

You Did More Than Carry My Books

JOHN W. SCHLATTER

ark was walking home from school one day when he noticed the boy ahead of him had tripped and dropped all of the books he was carrying, along with two sweaters, a baseball bat, a glove, and a small tape recorder. Mark knelt down and helped the boy pick up the scattered articles. Since they were going the same way, he helped to carry part of the stuff. As they walked Mark discovered the boy's name was Bill, that he loved video games, baseball, and history, and that he was having lots of trouble with his other subjects and that he had just broken up with his girlfriend.

They arrived at Bill's home first and Mark was invited in for a Coke and to watch some television. The afternoon passed with a few laughs and some shared small talk, then Mark went home. They continued to see each other around school, had lunch together once or twice, then both graduated from junior high school. They ended up in the same high school where they had brief contacts over the years. Finally the long awaited senior year came and three weeks before graduation, Bill asked Mark if they could talk.

Bill reminded him of the day years ago when they had first met. "Did you ever wonder why I was carrying so many things home that day?" asked Bill. "You see, I cleaned out my locker because I didn't want to leave a mess for anyone else. I had stored away some of my mother's sleeping pills and I was going home to commit suicide. But after we spent some time together talking and laughing, I realized that if I had killed myself, I would have missed that time and so many others that might follow. So you see, Mark, when you picked up those books that day, you did a lot more. You saved my life."

CHOOSING

*In high school I have learned to
choose my friends by their character
and my socks by their color.*

*—Kyle Sandburg
Graduation speech, Mountain View High School*

Downhill Race

SHAUN SWARTZ
FROM *TREASURES 2: STORIES & ART BY STUDENTS IN OREGON*

Racer ready? Ten seconds."
I was in the starting gate looking out over the fog-covered course. I had been working all season for this one moment, and now it was here. I had gone over the course many times in my mind and I was ready. This was my first race of the season, a super giant slalom qualifier at Mt. Bachelor. I, being one of the better skiers, was expected to do well.

"Five, four, three, two, one, hup, hup, hup," was the starter's call. At the first "hup," off I took, careening out of the starting gate like a bolt of lightning. The top of the course was a crucial part. I was the ninety-second racer out of one hundred and four racers and it was all rutted and icy. Around the first turn I zoomed with smoothness. Now that I was on the course, my jitters had left. As I approached the second and third turn, I was thinking ahead to waterfall, the toughest part of the course. At waterfall, going at approximately fifty-five miles an hour, you had to go off an eight-foot cliff that was all rutted and icy, and make almost a forty-five-degree turn in the air in order to be able to hit the next gate at the right place. Many people had fallen there, but I was confident.

As I got ever closer to waterfall, I was going over the steps in my mind. I was supposed to absorb the jump as much as I could, and there was a left-hand turn after the cliff. I really had to be on my toes. As I passed the gate preceding waterfall, just as I was getting ready to absorb the jump, I caught an edge on one of the many monstrous ruts. I soared like an eagle, upside down over waterfall, finally hitting the hard ground all twisted up. As I continued sliding crazily down the hill, one of my skis popped off just as I hit the gate knocking it out of the snow. When I eventually screeched awkwardly to a stop some twenty feet below waterfall, I didn't know what was happening. My legs ached, my arms ached, my neck hurt—and most of all, I was mad. As my senses started to return, I just lay there on the cold snow, hearing the ski patrolman and the gate-keeper yelling to see if I was all right. When I didn't answer, the ski patrolman quickly skied down to where I was to see if I was OK.

"What's your name, son?" he asked me.

"Shaun," I replied.

"Well, Shaun, that was the best crash of the day. What happened? Was it a rut?"

"I think so. Maybe I caught an edge."

"Yes, that could have happened too. Will you want me to call a snow-mobile to take you to the bottom, or are you just going to ski?"

"I'll take the ride if it isn't too much trouble," I replied dazedly.

In no time at all, they had the snowmobile up there and I was all strapped in with my skis next to me.

"So, Shaun, where do you want me to take you?" asked the driver.

"I'd really appreciate it if you could take me down to the bottom of the course," I answered.

As he drove me back down the hill, many questions raced through my mind. What happened? How did I do this? How am I going to explain this to my friends back at home who are expecting me to do well?

"Well, here you go, Shaun, the bottom of the course."

"Yeah, thanks a lot," I replied gratefully.

"Better luck next time," he said over his shoulder as he drove off.

"Thanks," I muttered feebly.

I took my skis over to the scoreboard and watched the last few racers to see how the rest of my team had done. As I approached the waiting area, there waiting to see his score was Chris.

Chris and I had been friends for many years. When I first moved here, I didn't really know anybody. Then Chris moved in exactly one mile away from our house. For about four summers, all we ever did was mess around at each other's house. We played basketball, and football, went swimming, wrestled, but most of all we skied. Chris and I were both heavily into skiing, and we had been racing together for several years.

Chris was a really cool guy. He was pretty skinny and very small. He had brown hair and blue eyes. In fact, he and I looked similar, the only differences being that I had brown eyes and was a little bigger.

"So, Chris, how did you feel on the course?" I asked.

"Pretty good. I think I could have done a little better, though. Too bad you crashed. What happened?"

"I'm not too sure. I must have done something," I answered.

"It sure is lucky for me that you crashed."

"Why is that?"

"Because usually you beat me, and I never get the recognition that you do because you are the better racer," he answered.

"It does feel kind of weird not winning. Now I understand how you guys always feel. You know, I always took winning for granted. I didn't really know what it felt like to lose or how much joy there really is in winning. I always thought, 'Wow, big deal, I won. Same old thing.'"

"Well, if it was so boring, why did you keep on racing?"

"No, I didn't say it was boring. I love to race and I love to win. I just didn't realize that there is another side to winning," I replied.

Just then Chris's score was posted. We quickly rushed over to see what place he had gotten since now all the racers had finished. When he found his name and discovered that he had won, he nearly knocked over the scoreboard in joy.

"Shaun, I can't believe this. This is the first race that I have ever won! I have always come in second or third!" he exclaimed.

When I saw the brightness in his manner, the wide smile that cracked across his face, the newly installed energy that was practically impossible to withhold, I knew he deserved that win. It was his turn.

"Thank you soooooo much for crashing. You made my dream come true!"

"Hey, what are friends for?" I answered.

When you're used to winning and find yourself at that place where you've lost, watch for the reward that you never allowed yourself to notice, one that can be so much more satisfying—the real winner's face.

My Name is Ike

GARY PAULSEN
FROM *MY LIFE IN DOG YEARS*

Much of my childhood in Thief River Falls, Minnesota, was excruciatingly lonely. Family troubles, devastating shyness, and a complete lack of social skills ensured a life of solitude. Hunting was not only my opening into a world of wonder, it was my salvation.

From the age of twelve, I lived, breathed, existed to hunt and fish. On school days I would hunt in the morning and evening. On Fridays I would head into the woods, often for the entire weekend.

Still, I had not learned to love solitude as I do now. I would see something beautiful—the sun through the leaves; a deer moving through dappled light—and I would want to point and say to someone, "Look!" But there was no one there.

Then I met Ike.

It was the beginning of duck season. I got up at 3 A.M. and walked from our apartment four blocks to the railroad yard, then across the Eighth Street bridge. There I dropped to the riverbank and started walking along the water into the woods.

In the dark it was hard going. After a mile and a half I was wading in swamp muck and went to pull myself up the bank to harder ground.

The mud was as slick as grease. I fell, then scrabbled up the bank again, shotgun in one hand and grabbing at roots with the other. I had just gained the top when a part of the darkness detached itself, leaned close to my face, and went "woof."

Not "arf" or "ruff" or a growl, but "woof."

For half a second I froze. Then I let go of the shrub and fell back down the incline. On the way down the thought hit: bear.

I clawed at my pockets for shells and inserted one into my shotgun. I was aiming when something about the shape stopped me.

Whatever it was had remained sitting at the top of the bank, looking down at me. There was just enough dawn to show a silhouette. It was a dog. A big dog, a black dog, but a dog.

I lowered the gun and wiped the mud out of my eyes. "Who owns you?" I asked. The dog didn't move, and I climbed the bank again. "Hello!" I called into the woods. "I have your dog here!"

There was nobody.

"So you're a stray." But strays were shy and usually starved; this dog, a Labrador, was well-fed and his coat was thick. He stayed near me.

"Well," I said. "What do I do with you?" On impulse I added, "You want to hunt?"

He knew that word. His tail hammered the ground and he wiggled, then moved off along the river.

I had never hunted with a dog before, but I started to follow. It was light enough now to shoot, so I kept the gun ready. We had not gone fifty yards when two mallards exploded out of some thick grass near the bank and started across the river.

I raised the gun, cocked it, aimed just above the right-hand duck and squeezed the trigger. There was a crash, and the duck fell into the water.

When I shot ducks over the river before, I had to wait for the current to bring the body to shore. This time was different. With the smell of the powder still in the air, the dog was off the bank in a great leap. He hit the water swimming, his shoulders pumping as he churned the surface in a straight line to the dead duck. He took it gently in his mouth, turned and swam back. Climbing the bank, he put the duck by my right foot, then moved off a couple of feet and sat.

It was fully light now, and I could see that the dog had a collar and tag. I petted him—he let me, in a reserved way—and pulled his tag to the side to read it.

My name is Ike.

That's all it said. No address, no owner's name.

"Well, Ike"—his tail wagged—"I'd like to thank you for bringing me the duck."

And that was how it started.

For the rest of the season, I hunted the river early every morning. I'd come across the bridge, start down the river and Ike would be there. By the middle of the second week, I felt as if we'd been hunting with each other forever.

When the hunting was done, he'd trot back with me until we arrived at the bridge. There he would sit, and nothing I did would make him come farther.

I tried waiting to see where he would go, but when it was obvious I wasn't going to leave, he merely lay down and went to sleep. Once I left him, crossed the bridge and then hid in back of a building to watch. He stayed until I was out of sight, then turned and trotted north along the river and into the woods.

If the rest of his life was a mystery, when we were together we became fast friends. I'd cook an extra egg sandwich for him, and when there were no ducks, we would talk. That is, I would talk. Ike would sit, his enormous head resting on my knee, his huge brown eyes looking up at me while I petted him and told him of all my troubles.

On the weekends when I stayed out, I would construct a lean-to and make a fire. Ike would curl up on the edge of my blanket. Many mornings I'd awaken to find him under the frost-covered blanket with me, his breath rumbling against my side.

It seemed Ike had always been in my life. Then one morning he wasn't there. I would wait in the mornings by the bridge, but he never showed again. I thought he might have been hit by a car or his owners might have moved away. But I could not learn more of him. I mourned him and missed him.

I grew and went into the crazy parts of my life, the mistakes a young man could make. Later I got back into dogs, sled dogs, and ran the Iditarod race across Alaska.

After my first run I came back home to Minnesota with slides of the race. A sporting goods store in Bemidji had been one of my sponsors, and one evening I gave a public slide show.

There was an older man sitting in a wheelchair, and I saw that when I told how Cookie, my lead dog, had saved my life, his eyes teared up and he nodded.

When the event was over, he wheeled up and shook my hand.

"I had a dog like your Cookie—a dog that saved my life."

"Oh, did you run sleds?"

He shook his head. "No, not like that. I lived up in Thief River Falls when I was drafted to serve in the Korean War. I had a Labrador retriever that I raised and hunted with. Then I was wounded—lost the use of my legs. When I came back from the hospital, he was waiting. He spent the rest of his life by my side.

"I would have gone crazy without him. I'd sit for hours and talk to him…" He faded off, and his eyes were moist again. "I still miss him."

I looked at him, then out the store window. It was spring and the snow was melting outside, but I was seeing a thirteen-year-old and a Lab sitting in a duck blind in the fall.

Thief River Falls, he said—and the Korean War. The time was right, and the place.

"Your dog," I said. "Was he named Ike?"

The man smiled and nodded. "Why, yes. But how…Did you know him?"

That was why Ike had not come back. He had another job.

"Yes," I said, turning to him. "He was my friend."

Diamonds

IRENE SOLA'NGE MCCALPHIN
FROM *FRIENDS*

can't wait. After nine years it is finally over. Freedom! Sweet freedom!" Raymond shouted, almost colliding with me as he ran up the steps of the Saint Anthony of Padua church. I glanced at him sharply. "Come on, Irene, you've been here as long as I have. I know that you're jumping for joy." He put an arm around my shoulders and smiled. His whole face lit up under his mass of straight, light brown hair. Red flushed into his cheeks and his green eyes sparkled. "I forgot how hard you cried yesterday. Still a little sentimental, huh? It's not in your nature to cry."

I tried to walk away from him, but he had his arm securely around my shoulders and every step I took, he took with me. I was embarrassed enough without his teasing. Yesterday our class had rehearsals for graduation, and I ended up crying so uncontrollably that even he was moved to sympathize.

That night I had called another friend on the phone and ended up crying again. After I stopped crying and she was sure that I was all right, she began fussing about how everyone had called her and done the same thing and how if she could have gotten through the phone line she would have slapped every one of them. I can't say I was shocked about it, Jackie was always on the rough side.

I snapped back to the present when Raymond tore away and began running after the other boys on their way home. Regretfully they all stopped, and Aquiles shouted, "Hurry up, Medusa, before we leave you." He liked to make fun of my hair, which I wore in braids. I tried not to blush at his words, but even through my dark skin it showed.

For the last two years, I was the only girl in an all-boy group that walked home from school together. I had to listen to all their pickup lines and the gory details of fights and movies. Sometimes they would stop halfway home to play football.

Before I reached them, I heard fake sobbing. And when I caught up to them, the sobs got louder. I felt sure that I would never miss them. For the remainder of the walk, which took five minutes but seemed like thirty, I promised myself that I would not cry again until after graduation tomorrow night. I only had a few hours to go.

Before we processed in for the ceremony, some of the boys made a bet on who would cry first. Needless to say, they all had their money on me.

During the ceremony I looked around at some of my friends. Elizabeth, with her long red hair and green eyes, who pushed me to do my best no matter what. Marcelo, who had the dark hair that I always wanted. He was always there to give me good advice, even though half the time he didn't realize what he was saying. And Thanh, with her slanted, dark, mischievous eyes that always saw my mistakes and made sure that I would never forget them. I could hardly believe that all the years had gone by so quickly. All the jokes and tears, all the fights and make ups. We tried to get away with some of the craziest things, and often did.

One by one a name was called, one by one someone that I held dear was gone. One by one we would set out on whatever path God led us on, even though it now meant traveling alone.

Friends are like newly found diamonds covered in dirt and coal. You will never know their beauty until you have chipped away the cover with tools of love and understanding. Inside, something wonderful but different awaits. Each possesses a love that can cut through fear, racism, and pain with a light so brilliant that it is not limited to only one color but includes the entire spectrum. And I can say with a good heart that I am rich beyond imagination.

LET THEM KNOW

As our high-speed world asks you
to log on, and e-mail a friend,
I'm asking you to talk to your friends,
hug them, let them know you are there for them.

—Sasha Sulkosky
Graduation speech, Mountain View High School

The Friendly Rival

BRUCE NASH AND ALLAN ZULLO
FROM *GREATEST SPORTS STORIES NEVER TOLD*

Track star Jesse Owens stared in disbelief at the flag signaling that he had fouled in his long-jump attempt. It was his second miss, leaving the world-record holder only one more chance to qualify for the finals in the 1936 Olympics.

The distance was just 23 feet, 5½ inches. Owens' world-record jump earlier that year was much longer—26 feet, 8¼ inches. But in the Olympic preliminaries, he had failed twice at the shorter distance. One more miss and Owens would be eliminated from the long jump.

Then, just when things seemed darkest, help came from an unexpected source—his main competitor! He was Germany's Lutz Long, the only jumper in the field with a shot at beating Owens.

The dramatic meeting of the African-American and the German hero is one of the great untold stories of the 1936 Olympics held in Berlin, Germany. Back then, German dictator Adolf Hitler and his followers disliked blacks and believed that whites were superior. Hitler hoped the Berlin Games would prove that white athletes were better than nonwhites.

115

But Owens, a student from Ohio State, proved the madman wrong. Jesse stunned Hitler and his Nazi followers by winning four gold medals in the 1936 Olympics. But without Lutz Long's unselfish sportsmanship, Owens would never have won a gold medal for the long jump.

Jesse had entered the two-hundred-meter race and the long jump even though both events were being held at about the same time. He started the day by running two qualifying heats for the two-hundred-meter race. Still in his sweatsuit, Owens then jogged to the infield section where the long-jump competition was just getting underway.

Because he was late in arriving, Jesse was unaware that competitive jumping had already started. He took a practice run down the runway and half-heartedly leaped into the pit. To his shock, the officials in charge said he fouled and counted his warm-up jump as his first of three attempts to qualify.

Rattled by the officials' decision, and still winded from the two-hundred-meter sprints he had just run, Owens tried too hard on his second attempt. He misjudged the takeoff spot—and fouled again! Jesse was now one jump away from being eliminated in his best event.

That's when a tall, blond German tapped Owens on the shoulder and introduced himself, in English, as Lutz Long—the German long jumper who had already qualified for the afternoon finals. The son of sharecroppers and the German athlete chatted for a few minutes. Long, who didn't believe in Hitler's absurd theories on white superiority, then offered to help Jesse.

"Something must be bothering you," Long told him. "You should be able to qualify with your eyes closed."

Owens explained that he hadn't known his first jump counted as a qualifying attempt and, in his eagerness to make up for the mistake, he overcompensated and missed his takeoff point on his second try.

"Since the distance you need to qualify isn't that difficult, make a mark about a foot before you reach the foul line," Long told Jesse. "Use that as your jump-off point. That way you won't foul."

Owens thanked his rival. Jesse then dug a mark with his foot in the grass next to the runway about a foot short of the foul line. Minutes later, he soared into his third and final jump—and qualified by more than two feet.

But the drama wasn't over.

That afternoon, the American and the German dueled in a classic Olympic showdown for the long-jump gold medal.

Owens' first jump set an Olympic record of 25 feet, 5½ inches. Then he bettered that mark with a leap of 25 feet, 10 inches. But Long responded to the challenge. On his next-to-last attempt, he thrilled thousands of fellow Germans in the huge stadium by matching Owens' record-setting jump.

Now it was Jesse's turn. The American champion answered with another record-smashing leap, this time 26 feet, 3¾ inches. Long needed a superhuman last effort. Trying to put everything into his jump, Long overran the board and fouled. Jesse Owens had won the gold medal!

Jesse still had another jump coming. He was so pumped up that he leaped 26 feet, 5¼ inches, breaking the Olympic record for the third time in three jumps.

With a scowling Adolf Hitler watching grimly from his box, the first person to throw his arms around Owens and congratulate him was Lutz Long.

Years later, Jesse recalled that moment when the two Olympic heroes stood arm in arm as friends: "You could melt down all the medals and cups I have and they wouldn't match the 24-carat friendship I felt for Lutz Long at that moment."

Long and Owens became good friends and wrote to each other even during World War II when Lutz was a lieutenant in the German army. In one battlefield letter to Jesse in 1943, Long wrote, "I hope we can always remain best of friends despite the differences between our countries." It was the last letter Owens ever received from Lutz. Just days after it was written, Jesse's good friend and track rival was killed in battle.

Jesse stayed in touch with Long's family, and several years after the war, he received a touching letter from Lutz's son, Peter, who was now twenty-two years old. In his letter, Peter said he was getting married. "Even though my father can't be here to be my best man, I know who he would want in his place. He would want someone that he and his entire family admired and respected. He would want you to take his place. And I do, too."

So Jesse Owens flew to the wedding in Germany and proudly stood at the side of the son of Lutz Long—a great friend and Olympic athlete who placed sportsmanship ahead of winning.

What's the Big Deal?

JULIE BERENS
from *WWJD Stories for Teens*

Who would have thought that a copy of *Gone with the Wind* could teach me a lesson about honesty and respect. That's what happened though when I lent my copy of the novel to my best friend, Christine.

"Please, Katie, I'll take good care of it," Christine said. "Pleeeease!"

I'll admit I'm crazy about my book collection, which includes an old copy of *Gone with the Wind* that my grandmother gave to me.

"Well, okay," I reluctantly agreed, knowing books weren't that important to Christine. But she's my best friend, and I felt like I had to say "yes."

Over the next few days, Christine kept me filled in on her progress through the story.

"Scarlett just married that wimp Charles!" she told me as we boarded the school bus one morning. "How could she?"

"Take good care of the book," was my usual reply every time she came to me with a report. She'd nod, but I wondered if she really heard me.

Christine not only kept me up-to-date about what page she was on in *Gone with the Wind,* but she also filled me in on the latest happenings at school.

"How do you find out this stuff?" I'd asked her in shock one day after hearing the latest story about Patty Speers, a cheerleader at our school. Christine shrugged. "I just keep my ears open."

Sometimes I wondered why my Christian friend was so interested in other people's lives. "I don't hurt anyone," Christine would say when I questioned her about the gossiping. "Besides I only tell a few people."

I wasn't sure who those few people were or exactly how many "a few" included, but I learned to shrug off Christine's wagging tongue even though I continued to listen to her. There are worse sins, I reasoned. Or so I thought.

A few weeks later Christine called me on the phone with more news about Patty. "She's pregnant!"

"What!" I could believe it about some other girls at our school, but not Patty. "You must have heard wrong."

"No, I didn't," she insisted. "Suzanne and Marcia were in the restroom talking about Patty and about babies. I distinctly heard her and Marcia say that Patty was expecting."

"What else did they say?"

"I don't know. I couldn't hear anything else."

I hung up with Christine and decided to call Robin, who's good friends with Patty. As I was dialing, my older brother Mark walked through the family room and into the kitchen to get a snack. He stood there as I talked to Robin.

"I heard that Patty's pregnant. Do you think it could be true?"

Robin said that she hadn't spent much time with Patty in the last few months because Patty was so busy with her new boyfriend. We talked a while longer and then I hung up. I still didn't have my answer.

"What are you doing?" Mark asked. I told him about Christine's call.

"Do you really think you should be calling these people?" he asked in that know-it-all voice that older brothers use.

"I'm trying to find out if the story's true." I dialed another number.

Mark looked at me funny but didn't say anything else. He left the room shaking his head.

The next day as we got on the bus, Christine told me she had about fifty pages to go. My thoughts were on Patty, but it didn't stop me from reminding Christine to be careful with my book.

That day at school the halls were full of whispers about Patty's pregnancy. "Is she or isn't she?" The question seemed to bounce off the walls and echo in the stairwells. The fact that Patty was absent only fueled the speculation.

Right before dinner that night, Christine showed up with my copy of *Gone with the Wind.* "What a fantastic book!" she said as she handed it to me.

As soon as I took it I could tell there was something wrong. The book fell limply backwards as I opened it.

As I turned the pages I could see where Christine had turned down corners to help her keep her place. The back cover of the book held a big coffee ring. "My dad couldn't find a coaster, so he set his mug down on the book," Christine explained. "The bottom of the mug must have been wet. I'm sorry about that."

"Christine, I asked you a million times to take care of this book!" I said. As my voice rose, Mark came out of his bedroom to see what the commotion was about. "If you can't take care of other people's things, you shouldn't ask to use them. You know how much my books mean to me."

Christine looked stunned. "I-I-I'm sorry," she stammered and hurried out the door to escape my tirade.

"Some people have no respect for other people's things," I muttered under my breath as I headed for my room.

"It's funny hearing you say that," Mark commented.

"And what's so funny about it? I told her to take care of my book, and she ruined it."

"Kind of like the two of you ruining Patty's reputation with your story about her being pregnant."

"Now wait a minute, I didn't spread that story. Christine called me, and I just called a few people to see if it was true."

"If that's what you were interested in why didn't you call Patty and ask her?" Mark demanded. "No, you didn't care enough about her to do that. You're just trying to hide your gossiping by acting like you care about Patty's welfare. Well, you're not fooling anyone."

I stood there taking in what Mark was saying.

"Maybe you need to think about it," he said, coming over and taking the book out of my hand. "This is just a thing, a book. So what if Christine turned some pages down or tore some of them or even spilled coffee on it. That's no big deal. But spreading rumors about someone being pregnant and hurting her reputation—now that is!"

Mark handed the book back to me. "I talked to Patty's mom today after school. Apparently Patty's expecting a new niece or nephew in the next few days. Her sister, Tina, is pregnant with her second child. Apparently Christine didn't hear the whole conversation."

I went to my room and closed the door. I laid on my bed and opened *Gone with the Wind*. Mark was right. A brown mark on a few pieces of paper shouldn't matter but the stain of doubt and suspicion that I'd left on Patty's reputation did.

I closed the book and put it back on the shelf, resolving that tomorrow I'd talk to Patty. On paper or in life, stains are hard to remove.

Happy Camper

ELESHA HODGE
FROM *CAMPUS LIFE* MAGAZINE

So, Elesha, are you excited about the Florida trip?"

"Joseph, get that video camera out of my face."

"Aw, c'mon. Sand, sun, hanging out with your friends…"

"Joseph, I mean it. Don't make me hurt you."

"…three whole days in beautiful Orlan—"

The tape fuzzes at this point. Joseph managed to scamper up the bus aisle before I had a chance to grab the camera and pitch it out the window. Barely.

I was anything *but* excited about the Florida trip. In fact, I was the only person in my high school show choir who had voted against it. I wanted to do a musical instead, but I was at the mercy of the majority. They wanted to try their luck in a big Disney sponsored choir competition. My personal motto for the trip became, *They can make me come along, but they can't make me like it.*

I had taken a twenty-four hour bus trip before. I mean, I knew the drive from Indiana to Florida was long, but I didn't begin to understand how long until the guys in choir opened up their bags and started pulling out wigs, gorilla masks, sound effects tapes, a fake arm and...you get the idea. The hours crawled by at roughly the speed of fingernails growing.

Somewhere near the Kentucky border, I attempted to escape my waking nightmare by falling asleep. Bad move. I woke up in Georgia covered in shaving cream, suntan lotion, toothpaste and shampoo. Too "mature" to even try to beat the guys at their own game, I sat out the rest of the trek in sticky silence.

Somehow, we did eventually make it to the DoubleTree Hotel in sunny Orlando. Only it wasn't sunny. In fact, it was downright frigid. I quickly discovered how tough it was to "bundle up" in shorts, T-shirts and a swimsuit. The best I could do was pile on every single article of clothing in my suitcase and hang out in my room watching an Agatha Christie movie on PBS.

The other members of the choir spent most of the night in the hallway. I'd occasionally hear a shout, a crash, or a guitar chord. I didn't know what they were doing out there, and I didn't care. I was half-tempted to call hotel security to shut them up.

The next day was cold, windy, and still mostly dark when I woke up. I rolled out of bed and suited up for song-and-dance fever.

I couldn't have designed uglier costumes if I'd tried. Itchy nylons, clunky shoes, and gold, shimmery, short jumpsuits that didn't even fit right. Our director thought they looked "flashy and today," whatever that meant. I thought we looked like *Star Trek* rejects.

When we got to the scene of the choir competition, we were immediately ushered into a band room to warm up and wait. The other groups were in that building somewhere, so a bunch of the guys in the group went on a reconnaissance mission to scout them out.

"They have a full brass section!" reported the guitarist in our meager five piece back up band, "And three saxes!"

"I heard one of the groups warming up. They sound *good.*"

"They were already smiling—and they weren't even in the auditorium yet!"

"I heard one group talking about how this is so much smaller than some other competition they won. Are we the only group that's never competed before?"

Yes, we were the only group that had never competed. And it showed in our performance. What I saw from my spot in the third row of dancers was disaster. Arms flailed everywhere. People turned and crashed into each other when the weren't supposed to be turning at all. One girl got whapped by an umbrella. (Yes, we really were dancing with sequined umbrellas. Don't even try to picture it.)

Then, incredibly, it all got worse. The guitarist got off by a measure in the middle of our third song. Half the group went with him, while the other half kept following the rest of the band. It took about sixteen bars of muddled words and missed cues for everyone to get back on track.

"That was awful!" my friend Leah choked out when we'd finally left the stage.

Well, it certainly wasn't good. But I didn't say that because that's not what she needed to hear. She needed to hear, "Yeah, we made some mistakes, but we were trying really hard. And it's our first competition. We'll do better next time." Like I could tell her that, after all my griping and negativity. I didn't say anything.

When we finally climbed into the bus and started driving north, I saw something that made me feel even worse: the video. There was a VCR on board, and Joseph thought that maybe showing his masterpiece would help people forget about our last-place finish.

Most of the tape was really pretty amusing. Some of the stuff from the bus ride was kind of funny. The people who'd play in the hotel hall while I watched PBS looked like they were having a great time. And right up until the chaotic mess in the third song—everybody groaned while we relived *those* moments—our performance at the competition wasn't half-bad.

In fact, it was probably the best show we'd ever put on. Most of the glitches I'd seen on stage weren't too noticeable from the audience. We'd been bad enough to finish last, but not so bad that we needed to lock ourselves in the costume closet when we got home.

What stuck out on the tape as I watched it was *me*. I was the most unfun person on that trip. When I appeared on the video, I was always either scowling or complaining. The funniest parts of the video didn't include me at all.

One of the last things we did before arriving back was hand out awards. "Worst excuse for being late," "Best souvenir," that sort of thing. All I managed to win was the very sarcastically titled "Happy Camper Award." And I still have it in my scrapbook, reminding me that nothing ruins an experience like a bad attitude.

i Got What i Needed

BILL FARREL
FROM *GOD'S VITAMIN "C" FOR THE SPIRIT OF MEN*

Two weeks before the beginning of my senior year, I moved to a new school and entered a new basketball program. At the beginning of the year I found that I was a bit of a novelty because I was new, but as the season wore on, I discovered that I didn't fit very well in the system run by this new coach. As a result, I spent more and more time sitting on the bench. The agony was driven into my heart as weekly I received the newspaper from the town where I was supposed to play my senior year. The team in that town was winning their league title while the team I was on was in the middle of the pack. The team I left behind would have had me as the starting point guard while the team I was on was enjoying my contribution in practice only.

In the midst of this struggle I became friends with Allen. Allen believed in my abilities and was seeking ways to encourage me because he knew I was playing below my ability. Halfway through the season he said, "I've got a deal for you. If you score in double figures in any game this season I will buy you a steak dinner."

That was the new motivation I needed to work hard again. I began to give it my all in practice, again thinking I would get another shot. But the opportunity was slow in developing. In the next six games I played a total of ten minutes. Allen sensed the dilemma I was in so he modified the deal.

"If you score in double figures for the rest of the season combined, I will buy you a steak dinner."

I took his challenge to heart with joy and anticipation. I knew we would not win a championship. I knew we would not even get to the play-offs. But with six games left in the season, I thought I would at least have a personal victory if I could score enough points. The next three games saw me with three-and-a-half minutes of playing time so my hope of meeting his challenge was dissipating. In one last desperate attempt to encourage me, Allen modified his offer one more time.

"Bill, if you score even one basket, I will buy you a steak dinner."

With three games left to play, I was a man on a mission. My dreams of a championship season were history but my desire to give Allen a chance to make good on his offer was very much alive. In the first game, I played thirty seconds. In the second game, I played sixteen seconds. No points, no victory.

My opportunity came in the last game of the season. The coach put me in with one minute and thirty-five seconds left in the game. We were trailing by fifteen points with no hope of winning. I was frantically running around the court trying to steal the ball. Finally my chance came. With twelve seconds left in the game a teammate and I trapped a player at half court. I stole the ball with six seconds left on the clock and went the length of the court for a lay-up. With two seconds left in the game the ball fell through the net. We had just lost by thirteen points but I was running down the side of the court pointing to my friend who was sitting in the top row of the stands.

I was jumping up and down like we had just won the league championship, shouting, "You owe me, Allen. You owe me."

Allen was on his feet, pointing back to me, shouting, "You did it, Bill. You did it!"

What I wanted was a championship season my senior year in high school that I could brag about for the rest of my life. What I needed was a friend like Allen who would let me know I was valuable because of who I am not just for what I do. I didn't get what I wanted, but I got what I needed—a true friend.

Who We Are

We've grown to cherish one another,
not for what we look like, or how we act, or how we dress,
but for who we are and who we are becoming.

—*Aubrey Leigh Denzer*
Graduation speech, Sisters High

Cincinnati

HOLLY MELZER
FROM *FRIENDS*

Vanessa and I met at dance class six years ago and have been close friends ever since. She lives in Gahanna, I live in Reynoldsburg, and with our busy social lives we see each other less and less. We used to have to badger our parents for rides to each other's house. We couldn't wait until we got our licenses so we could drive places ourselves. We joked around about driving to Cincinnati just for the fun of it with her radio blaring and windows rolled down, hair blowing in the breeze.

At first we had talked a few times, but I wouldn't say we were friends. I begged my mom to drop me off early and pick me up late so I could watch Vanessa dance. I sat on the floor with my nose pressed against the window, watching in admiration. She could do a triple pirouette in a third of a second. I got dizzy just watching her whirl around the room like a top that had just been let loose. I adored Vanessa.

When I was in sixth grade and Vanessa was in seventh, I picked her as my "big sister" for dance lines. She bought me the best presents and wrote me little notes spontaneously to make me feel better. She curled my hair at competitions, taught me how to put on makeup without looking like a clown, and how to talk to guys. She listened to my stories about my latest crushes. Most of all, she was always there when I needed her.

I moved up to her dance lines and classes, so we saw each other all the time. We became best friends. I lived at her house on weekends and vacations. We shared everything. We had half of our clothes in each other's closet, and toothbrushes in each other's bathroom. We told each other everything and went through so much together.

One day my mom dropped us off at Vanessa's house; we could hear her parents shouting before we even opened the door. Vanessa, a little embarrassed, turned a slight shade of red. I flashed a smile, grabbed their mail, and followed her quietly into her room where we sat for hours, ignoring the arguing and occasional shouts that came from the kitchen. Her parents never realized we had come in. We were lying on her bed when her dad yelled, "I want a divorce!" and her mom screamed, "Great!" I hugged weeping Vanessa, her lips moving silently with the word "divorce."

Vanessa spent that night at my house. We had stayed up late, so when my mom came in the room at 5:00 A.M. and turned the lights on, we were confused. All I heard was "Going to the hospital" as my mom closed the door.

Finally around 9:00 A.M., we heard the garage door open. Vanessa turned off the Bugs Bunny cartoon that we weren't really watching. We stared fearfully at each other. Mom walked slowly through the door, hung up her coat, and looked at us both. "Grandma died." Vanessa wrapped her arms around me, both of us with tears streaming down our face.

We're always there when we need each other most. Going to different schools has strained our friendship, but we've been through too much to throw it away because of a few inconveniences. We talk on the phone often and go out on weekends.

Vanessa still does little things to surprise me. Saturday she called at 9:00 A.M., saying she was coming over. When she arrived, I jumped in the car. "Where to?" I screamed above the blaring radio. "Cincinnati," she answered, laughing. I smiled as she peeled out of my driveway, our hair blowing in the breeze.

Our Friendship Tree

HARRISON KELLY

Friendships that last longest are the ones with the deepest roots. Those are the ones that mature into brotherhood.

In the third grade, I was still the new kid in school, only with a year's experience. Just twelve months before, my family moved into a suburb of Memphis named Frayser, a middle-class neighborhood instilled with a strong work ethic. But the residents were a little hesitant when it came to outsiders.

One day, a boy with a nervous look on his face came into our class for the first time. His name was Tom and his family had just moved from Nashville. You could tell he didn't like being the new kid, no more than I did.

Since the desk behind mine was the only one empty, the teacher assigned it to him. Knowing firsthand of the difficulty in getting to know people, I made the first effort. Soon we became best friends, a camaraderie that outlasted classes well into the summer.

Tom's house was a mile and a half from mine, near a large townhouse development in one of the quieter sections. I lived on the boulevard with its non-stop hurry. Even though we lived so far apart, our friendship grew.

We'd meet each other halfway, under a yellow oak that hung over the parking lot of the local Methodist church. The tree's mammoth size was legendary, with a trunk at least six feet around and branches as big as barrels. We called it Our Friendship Tree as it seemed to symbolize everything we felt about our mutual esteem.

It was a stopping point, a meeting place, a beginning and an ending. During that first summer, we met there, with baseball gloves in hand to plan our mornings and would depart every afternoon, resolved to return.

As the years marched before our eyes, it seemed like Our Friendship Tree was always there, watching our growth, guiding our paths. We walked under its orange leaves to Cub Scouts in the fall and first talked about girls while resting at the foot of its trunk. We met under its branches in tuxedos the night of our senior prom. When we wore our caps and gowns at our baccalaureate. Again, as we threw rice after our weddings. That tree seemed to be as much a part of our lives as the friendship itself.

As we became adults and parents, we moved away from Frayser. However, we still kept in touch with each other. One day, Tom called me out of the blue. He told me that lightning had struck Our Friendship Tree and had caused it to fall to the ground. I shed a tear as I realized its roots were really ours. Gone was a symbol of our childhood together, something never to be replaced.

Six months passed, then I read in the newspaper about a man that made writing pens from wood that had special meanings. As I read the article, I wished that I would have saved a piece from Our Friendship Tree. But as I read further, to my surprise, the man lived in Frayser! Maybe he had some wood from that old tree.

Sure enough, he did. The tree grew on the property of his old church and he had made pens for some in the congregation. When he said he had two pens left, I almost couldn't hold myself back.

I met Tom for lunch one afternoon and gave him one of the pens, as a symbol of our past and a promise to always be there in the future. I kept the other for myself and often reflect as I write, remembering my roots.

Encouragement

Things I've Learned Lately...

Smiles can make your day,
All little boys miss their mommies at bedtime,
The stars shine brighter when there is no moon,
And everyone has something that makes their heart glad.

God Has a Plan for Your Baby

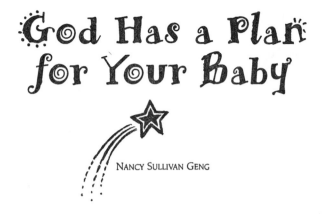

NANCY SULLIVAN GENG

The hospital room was wrapped in early morning darkness as bright flakes of November snow fell outside the window near my bed. My husband slept soundly on a cot that the nurses had set up, but I drifted in and out of restless sleep.

I kept recounting the previous night in fragments: labor...pain...a baby...a diagnosis.

Then slowly opening my eyes, I remembered the doctor's midnight words: "I'm sorry, Mr. and Mrs. Geng.... Our preliminary findings indicate that your baby has the symptoms and tendencies of Down's syndrome."

The digital clock on top of my suitcase clicked to 6:02 A.M. I was worn and tired. I wanted to sleep but unanswerable questions kept me from rest:

What did the future hold?

How would we tell our families?

Would our marriage adjust to the ongoing challenges of her disability?

Then, I heard a soft knocking sound. Turning my glance to the door, I saw the silhouette of a young pony-tailed girl in a pleated skirt, her outline shadowed by the dim lights of the hospital hallway.

As she moved closer, I brushed the sleep from my eyes to make out the face. It was Jessy. We smiled, simultaneously. As she sat down in a chair next to my bed, I called to mind memories from a September morning just the year before. I was newly graduated from college; it was the first day of my teaching career.

I had been assigned to Room 202, in a Catholic high school.

As the school bell sounded through the aging brick corridors, twenty-one sophomores entered my 8:00 A.M. homeroom, a fifteen-minute block of time that preceded scheduled classes, a time reserved for announcements and attendance.

The students were all girls, all uniformed in the black woolen pleats and white starched collars of an eighty-year tradition. Carrying backpacks weighted with college prep books, they squeaked to their desks in polished saddle shoes.

"I'm Mrs. Geng," I announced as I wrote my name on the blackboard.

Jessy, along with the other girls in the class, watched closely and whispered. I too was uniformed, but I knew that my navy blue tweeds and professional pumps could not conceal my youth and inexperience.

But as the mornings passed, those homeroom whispers found a voice in the brief conversations we began to exchange.

Sometimes we talked of academic pressures.

Other times, our topics were more lighthearted, especially on Monday mornings when the girls bantered about the weekend: basketball games, and slumber parties, dances and dresses and dates.

But somehow it always seemed that those homeroom conversations flowed into curious questions about my life:

Was the college I attended a good one?

What was my first date like?

How did I meet my young husband?

I never grew tired of their inquiries or sharing my life with them. They were like younger sisters eager for advice and insight. And though my college professors had warned against becoming "too friendly" with the students, I was honored to offer what little I had learned about life.

The year passed quickly. Then one spring morning in May, I came to homeroom clutching an ultrasound picture I had gotten from the doctor just a day earlier.

Revealing that I was three months pregnant, the girls cheered and began kidding me about maternity clothes and support hose. They agreed unanimously that surely it would be a girl.

Then as they gathered around my desk, I uncreased the black and white sonogram as I outlined the baby's heart and head and hands. The girls looked on in wonder and amazement, all except for Jessy. She stood back from the group, her blond pony-tailed hair framing a somber smile and blue eyes that hinted of secret sadness.

As homeroom ended with the sound of a bell, the girls rushed off to their first hour classes, but Jessy lingered behind.

"Mrs. Geng...can I talk to you?" she asked in almost a whisper.

"Sure," I said as I glanced at my teaching schedule; I was free until 9:00. We sat down in side-by-side desks.

"I'm pregnant too," she began, her eyes now welling up with tears.

"I'm almost four months along and I don't know what to do.... My mom is divorced. She's worked hard to afford my tuition. How am I going to tell her? What will she say? What will she do if I can't stay in school?"

For a moment, Jessy just covered her face with her hands. "It's okay Jessy...tell me more," I said.

When she gained her composure, she talked about the child's father, a star football player from the boy's school across the street.

"He's been nominated for an athletic scholarship.... We both know we're too young to get married, too young to take care of a baby.... I'm so scared, Mrs. Geng."

As I listened, I wasn't sure if she could receive the words I felt compelled to say, but I offered them nonetheless:

"Jessy," I began. "God has a plan for your baby. Don't ever forget that." As the last days of school approached, Jessy and I met often to talk.

During that time, Jessy told her mom about the pregnancy and found unforeseen compassion and comfort along with a loving coach to support her through birthing classes.

I, in turn, met with the principal to strategize how we as a school might help Jessy and her family during the remaining months of her pregnancy.

Much to Jessy's surprise, the school invited her to return to classes in the fall, even though her due date was scheduled for mid-October, just six weeks before mine.

All through the summer months, I thought of Jessy as I gathered gifts at baby showers and when I shopped for car seats and crib sheets.

Every time I felt the motions and movements of my baby, I couldn't help but visualize her meeting with social workers and signing adoption policies and paging through biographies of prospective parents.

Her plans and preparations for birth were so different than mine....

When the autumn days of early September arrived, Jessy greeted me in the doorway of Room 202. Wearing a plaid maternity top, blue jeans, and tennis shoes, she waved her class schedule and called out with a smile: "I'm in your homeroom again, Mrs. Geng!"

We tried to hug each other but found it impossible. After almost eight months of pregnancy, our stomachs were the same size. We laughed.

Four weeks later, Jessy delivered a healthy baby girl. After just a few days of recovery, she was back in homeroom neatly uniformed. There she showed me pictures of the baby she had given away, the daughter she had cradled in the hospital for a few short hours.

"I told her that I loved her, Mrs. Geng...."

Now, as the first snow of the season fell outside my hospital window, I too had given birth. Jessy had come to visit, to welcome my Down's syndrome daughter.

She had come in the early morning hours, before school, to offer me the words I had once offered her:

"Mrs. Geng," she began, "God has a plan for your baby. Don't ever forget that...."

I looked at her and smiled.

For so many months I had felt compelled to teach her to trust in God's plan. How well she had learned that lesson. She knew it by heart. Now trust was the tender lesson she could teach me.

It's been twelve years since that day. Just a few weeks back as I waited in my car at a corner stoplight, Jessy pulled up right next to me in a station wagon.

I waved. She honked.

There was a baby sleeping right next to her in a car seat. When the light changed, Jessy drove away, but my Down's syndrome daughter and her two younger sisters called out from the backseat, "Who was that, Mommy?"

I smiled.

"That was a teacher I once knew, one of my best."

T. J.

SUSAN CUNNINGHAM EUKER
FROM *HEART AT WORK*

i am a teacher. I don't think I actually knew that until spring of last year, even though I have been in the classroom for more than twenty years.

Until I met T. J., I was an educator. Not that there is anything wrong with being an educator—it is just different from being a teacher. It is perhaps more academic, more accountable to standardized state tests, more necessary to Scholastic Aptitude Test scores. Teaching is listening to the small voice in your heart that validates children the world has dismissed. It is sharing a part of yourself and in the process receiving back far more than you give.

T. J. changed it for me—big, blond, unkempt, antisocial, quiet, forgotten T. J. He taught me much about what I value about myself and how those values transfer to my students. He showed me what my profession is about.

T. J. sat in the very back of my classroom alone, isolated for one entire semester and, in spite of my efforts, did nothing—no assignments, no tests, no class work, no participation, no interest in much of anything. And he failed—flat.

I was curious about this unusual young man, and after checking confidential records in the guidance office, I discovered information that made the pieces of T. J.'s puzzle fit. He had lost his father by the seventh grade and had great difficulty getting along with his alcoholic mother throughout his teenage years. He had a brother who was severely limited, and there was indication of possible abuse of both children. T. J.'s mother was so verbally abusive to the school administrators that they had almost given up dealing with T. J.'s truancy.

T. J. lived in a painfully dysfunctional family. His low self-esteem became understandable to me; his reason for hurrying home each day after school became clearer; and his missing school frequently even became justifiable. I hurt for him.

Because my course is required for graduation from high school and because for some reason T. J. wanted to graduate, he was back in the spring semester of his senior year for one final try. I had my doubts. So did everyone else.

Things began that semester with T. J. withdrawing as he had done previously. But then as the class discussed self-esteem one day, something changed. I had my students tape blank pieces of paper on their backs, and I gave them five minutes to circulate around the room, find five people they did not know particularly well and write one positive thing they had noticed about that person on the sheet. After we sat down and discussed anxieties and feelings about completing this exercise, I asked them to write a paragraph describing themselves as others saw them and how they felt about what they had read. T. J. did as he was directed. I wondered why.

The next day, T. J. approached me after class and asked if he could present his personality collage to the class. I was agreeable, even though the collage had been due more than a month before and had been presented by the other students on a day when T. J. was truant. Frankly, I was curious, and I told T. J. that we would be delighted to see his collage.

When T. J. came to class the next day he had his collage with him and was prepared to explain it to the class. The other students had presented

143

elaborate posters with pictures, words, and mementos arranged artistically on various sizes and shapes of tag board. T. J.'s collage consisted of only one thing: three farming magazines connected to one another by a piece of baling rope. T. J. explained that farming was his family's business and baling twine was what held his life together. At the bottom of the three magazines was taped the piece of paper T. J. had worn the day we had done the self-esteem activity. Written on it were "kind," "funny," "pretty hair," "a nice person," and "caring."

I silently hung the collage in the front of the room for all to see. As T. J. returned to his seat that day he moved his chair up close to the last row of students. I fought back the tears and continued the lesson of the day. Sensing the privilege of experiencing T. J.'s presence, perhaps for the first time, the class remained silent. For T. J., it was the beginning of a connection.

T. J. graduated last June. Not only did he pass my class, but he also somehow passed twelfth grade social studies, the bane of every graduating senior. During the graduation ceremony, there was only one time when I felt the joy of that small voice in my heart—when T. J. received his diploma. I remembered the gift he had given me and my fourth-period class that semester, and I cried. As he passed me in the recessional that night, with his robes flying, his mortar board askew and his diploma held high in joyful celebration, he smiled, reached out, shook my hand...and winked.

I knew then I was a teacher. T. J. taught me that.

Information Please

PAUL VILLIARD
REPRINTED WITH PERMISSION FROM THE JUNE 1966 READER'S DIGEST
© 1966 BY THE READER'S DIGEST ASSN., INC.

When I was quite young, my family had one of the first telephones in our neighborhood. I remember well the polished oak case fastened to the wall on the lower stair landing. The shiny receiver hung on the side of the box. I even remember the number—105. I was too little to reach the telephone, but used to listen with fascination when my mother talked to it. Once she lifted me up to speak to my father, who was away on business. Magic!

Then I discovered that somewhere inside that wonderful device lived an amazing person—her name was "Information Please" and there was nothing she did not know. My mother could ask her for anybody's number; when our clock ran down, Information Please immediately supplied the right time.

My first personal experience with this genie-in-the-receiver came one day while my mother was visiting a neighbor. Amusing myself at the toolbench in the basement, I whacked my finger with a hammer. The pain was terrible, but there didn't seem to be much use crying because there was no one home to offer sympathy. I walked around the house sucking my throbbing finger, finally arriving at the stairway. The telephone! Quickly I ran for the footstool in the parlor and dragged it to the landing. Climbing up, I unhooked the receiver and held it to my ear. "Information Please," I said into the mouthpiece just above my head.

A click or two, and a small, clear voice spoke into my ear. "Information."

"I hurt my fingerrr—" I wailed into the phone. The tears came readily enough, now that I had an audience.

"Isn't your mother home?" came the question.

"Nobody's home but me," I blubbered.

"Are you bleeding?"

"No," I replied. "I hit it with the hammer and it hurts."

"Can you open your ice box?" she asked. I said I could.

"Then chip off a little piece of ice and hold it to your finger. That will stop the hurt. Be careful when you use the ice pick," she admonished. "And don't cry. You'll be all right."

After that, I called Information Please for everything. I asked for help with my geography and she told me where Philadelphia was, and the Orinoco—the romantic river I was going to explore when I grew up. She helped me with my arithmetic, and she told me that a pet chipmunk—I had caught him in the park just the day before—would eat fruit and nuts.

And there was the time that Petey, our pet canary, died. I called Information Please and told her the sad story. She listened, then said the usual things grown-ups say to soothe a child. But I was unconsoled: Why was it that birds should sing so beautifully and bring joy to whole families, only to end up as a heap of feathers feet up, on the bottom of a cage?

She must have sensed my deep concern, for she said quietly, "Paul, always remember that there are other worlds to sing in."

Somehow I felt better.

Another day I was at the telephone. "Information," said the now familiar voice.

"How do you spell fix?" I asked.

"Fix something? F-I-X."

At that instant my sister, who took unholy joy in scaring me, jumped off the stairs at me with a banshee shriek—"Yaaaaaaaaaa!" I fell off the stool, pulling the receiver out of the box by the roots. We were both terrified—Information Please was no longer there, and I was not at all sure that I hadn't hurt her when I pulled the receiver out.

Minutes later there was a man on the porch. "I'm a telephone repairman. I was working down the street and the operator said there might be some trouble at this number." He reached for the receiver in my hand. "What happened?"

I told him.

"Well, we can fix that in a minute or two." He opened the telephone box, exposing a maze of wires and coils, and fiddled for a while with the end of the receiver cord, tightening things with a small screwdriver. He jiggled the hook up and down a few times, then spoke into the phone. "Hi, this is Pete. Everything's under control at 105. The kid's sister scared him and he pulled the cord out of the box."

He hung up, smiled, gave me a pat on the head and walked out the door.

All this took place in a small town in the Pacific Northwest. Then, when I was nine years old, we moved across the country to Boston—and I missed my mentor acutely. Information Please belonged in that old wooden box back home, and I somehow never thought of trying the tall, skinny new phone that sat on a small table in the hall.

Yet as I grew into my teens, the memories of those childhood conversations never really left me; often in moments of doubt and perplexity I would recall the serene sense of security I had when I knew that I could call Information Please and get the right answer. I appreciate now how very patient, understanding, and kind she was to have wasted her time on a little boy.

A few years later, on my way west to college, my plane put down in Seattle. I had about half an hour between plane connections, and I spent fifteen minutes or so on the phone with my sister who lived there now, happily mellowed by marriage and motherhood. Then, really without thinking what I was doing, I dialed my hometown operator and said, "Information Please."

Miraculously, I heard again the small, clear voice I knew so well: "Information."

I hadn't planned this, but I heard myself saying, "Could you tell me, please, how to spell the word 'fix'?"

There was a long pause. Then came the softly spoken answer. "I guess," said Information Please, "that your finger must have healed by now."

I laughed. "So it's really still you. I wonder if you have any idea how much you meant to me during all that time...."

"I wonder," she replied, "if you know how much you meant to me? I never had any children, and I used to look forward to your calls. Silly, wasn't it?"

It didn't seem silly, but I didn't say so. Instead I told her how often I had thought of her over the years, and I asked if I could call her again when I came back to visit my sister after the first semester was over.

"Please do. Just ask for Sally."

"Good-bye, Sally." It sounded strange for Information Please to have a name. "If I run into any chipmunks, I'll tell them to eat fruit and nuts."

"Do that," she said. "And I expect one of these days you'll be off for the Orinoco. Well, good-bye."

Just three months later I was back again at the Seattle airport. A different voice answered, "Information," and I asked for Sally.

"Are you a friend?"

"Yes," I said. "An old friend."

"Then I'm sorry to have to tell you. Sally had only been working part-time in the last few years because she was ill. She died five weeks ago." But before I could hang up, she said, "Wait a minute. Did you say your name was Villiard?"

"Yes."

"Well, Sally left a message for you. She wrote it down."

"What was it?" I asked, almost knowing in advance what it would be.

"Here it is, I'll read it—'Tell him I still say there are other worlds to sing in. He'll know what I mean.'"

I thanked her and hung up. I did know what Sally meant.

A Student's Plea

MELISSA ANN BROECKELMAN

Teach me to strive for success; challenge me
Let fantasy become reality
Allow my well of knowledge to run deep
Develop this mind that I'll always keep
Give me instructions and provide a means
To see that the path isn't as it seems
Give me assurance and let me believe
That with persistence, my dreams I'll achieve
I want to prove no goal is out of reach
Show me the right direction, I beseech
Let me dissolve each mental boundary
So I can reach out and seize the victory
Push me to extents far beyond extremes
Do this, and you'll help me attain my dreams

Molder of Dreams

GUY RICE DOUD
FROM MOLDER OF DREAMS

Mr. Card was my sixth-grade teacher and my first male teacher. When I walked into class that first day, I was surprised to see a man in the room. I wondered if this man was a new janitor, but I guessed not because he had on dress slacks, a white shirt and a tie. I examined him. He looked too young to be a teacher.

By the time I had reached sixth grade, I was quite discouraged about school and life. I had learned I wasn't one of the brightest kids in class. I was horrible at math. My artwork had been left off the bulletin board. The teacher was always telling me that I had to keep a clean desk, and I just couldn't figure how Mary, who sat next to me, could keep her desk so organized. I sang too loud. No one ever picked me first while choosing teams for kickball. I was never the captain, and I had concluded I would never be the captain or one of the popular kids.

No one deliberately set out to teach me these things, and no one, except a few classmates who made fun of my size, ever purposely meant to hurt me. But I had come to believe I wasn't very good.

I was worried when I realized Mr. Card was going to be my teacher. Men aren't as nice as women, you know. Men are hard and don't have the sympathy women do. At least that's what I thought at the time. And I felt I needed someone who would have sympathy for me; Mr. Card didn't look like he would.

I studied him some more. He walked over to me, held out his hand and said, "Hi, I'm Mr. Card. Norm Card. I'm going to be your teacher."

I had never had a teacher shake my hand before, but I extended my hand and obliged.

"What's your name?" he asked.

"Guy Doud."

"Oh, I've heard about you."

Oh no, I thought. *You've heard that I'm no good at math or art, and that I don't like SRA boxes. You know I sing too loud and have a messy desk. You probably know about my mom and dad and that we're not very rich and we've never been to Disneyland or any place like that....*

But I've never found out what Mr. Card knew, and I've never asked him, because he treated me like somebody special. I guess he treated all the kids that way, but what mattered to me was the way he treated me, and it felt good.

Mr. Card was a first-year teacher, right out of college. He did things with us I didn't think teachers were allowed to do. He played with us at recess. He ran around and yelled like a big kid.

We had graduated from kickball to touch football, and Mr. Card was always on one of our teams. He was the quarterback. He didn't let us pick the teams. He divided us up, and he took turns playing for both teams.

One day when he was on my team he said, "Guy, I want you to go out for the pass. Go down the left side. Cut across. When you get to the middle, I'll hit you with the pass."

It gave me such confidence to know that Mr. Card trusted me enough to throw to me. I had come to believe that my role in football was to block, but Mr. Card was giving me my chance to be a receiver.

I lined up as he called the signals. I felt my heart beating in my head. I wanted to catch this ball. I wanted to prove that not just fast, skinny kids could be receivers. I could catch it, too.

The ball was centered. I was off like a slow train, but I was bound and determined to reach my destination.

Mr. Card was elusive in the backfield. Sometimes he would run around back there for what seemed like twenty minutes as we tried to touch him. Just when you thought you had him, he would jump out of the way. This was good as far as I was concerned, because as he was eluding would-be tacklers, I was starting my cut across the center of the playing field.

No one was paying much attention to me. My being a receiver had never been a part of anyone's game plan. It took everyone by surprise when Mr. Card unloaded the football and threw a strike right to me.

He threw it so hard that if one of the skinny kids had been catching the ball, it would have carried him an extra three yards. But it went through my hands, hit my belly, and was starting to bounce away when I pulled it in, smothering it in the folds of my stomach.

I caught it! I was so excited I forgot to run, and Marty quickly touched me. I've since wished we had been playing tackle football because I was so proud after catching that ball that I think I could have carried the entire sixth-grade class into the end zone.

I liked Mr. Card. He came by my desk to check my work, and as he looked it over, he rested his hand on my shoulder. His hand, although extremely heavy and causing me a great deal of anxiety, said, *I like you, Guy. You're okay.*

Sometimes I would raise my hand, kind of hoping that maybe Mr. Card would come by my desk. Maybe his hand would need a place to rest for a moment, and he would use my shoulder.

I worked hard for him, and he told me I was a good worker. I came to believe that maybe doing your best and working hard was even more important than being really smart and getting your artwork up on the bulletin board.

The last week of class Mr. Card handed out awards. It was a full-blown ceremony. He seemed to find something to give everyone. He even gave an award for the person who had to ride the farthest on the bus every day. He got down to the two last awards and said he thought these awards were the two most important of all, for they would go to the hardest working girl and the hardest working boy.

I wondered who would win those awards. I surveyed the room. I figured either Mary or Linda would win for the girls, and I bet probably Sam or Danny would win for the boys.

"The award for the hardest working boy in Mr. Card's sixth-grade class goes to Guy Doud."

I heard him say it, but I didn't believe it.

"Guy, come on up and get your award."

I rose from my desk. I was the only one with a steel desk. Mr. Hill had gone to the junior high and brought back a steel desk for me after I had broken my wooden one. I had rocked backward in it, and one of the legs had broken.

"Hardest Working Boy in Mr. Card's Sixth-Grade Class"—that's what the certificate said. Just a plain piece of mimeographed paper; but it couldn't have meant more to me if it had been a gold statue.

My mom felt the same way, because she left it on the door of the refrigerator, until I took it down about three weeks into seventh grade.

Chasing Rainbows

DE'LARA KHALILI
FROM *CAMPUS LIFE* MAGAZINE

We there yet, Papau?"

"No, hon, not yet."

Wet grass clung to my arms as I waded through a field of shoulder-high weeds following a path cut by a pair of big leather boots.

"We there yet, Papau?"

"Should be home in a little while. You gettin' tired, Lora?"

"No way." I warily plucked a June bug from my pink sweater and tiny twigs from my hair. "I could walk all day."

I was dead tired—tired of the weeds, of the bees buzzing an anthem around my head, of climbing hills, of everything that most five-years-olds like myself hated. But I was never tired of walking with Papau, I loved him. I tried to look up at him, but the first shafts of morning sunlight blinded me. The sun was trying to pierce sinister black thunderheads from morning's storm.

"We there yet, Papau?" My voice whined high and shrill.

"Why, Lora, I thought you liked walkin' with your ole Papau?" His tanned leathered face threatened a laugh, his warm blue eyes smiled.

"I do, but..." I collapsed to the wet spongy ground and began to cry. "But I wanna go home.... I wanna watch cartoons.... I WAAANT MOMMA." Salty tears rolled down my face.

He looked down at his dirty little granddaughter lying in the weeds, crying and slapping angrily at flies. He laughed. "Well, that beats all I ever heard, little girl." He knelt down and gathered me into his arms, patting me gently on my back. "The house is just over yonder a ways, Lora."

I cried loudly on his shoulder as he waded through the weeds. But then he stopped, and I could hear a sharp intake of breath.

"Well, looky there, Lora!" He pried me from his shoulder and pointed into the valley.

I turned around and gasped between sobs. "I never saw one this close."

"Something else, ain't it, girl?"

Bursting through an angry cluster of clouds, a crescent of color arched gracefully to earth and seemed to rest in the bottom of a small vale. I was entranced. I had seen a rainbow before, of course, but never this close. I reached for it as though I could plunge my hands into the shimmering curves and carry a piece away. I scrambled out of Papau's arms, knocking his hat off and practically pulling him to the ground.

"Whoa, where you going, gal?" He slapped his hat back on his head and laughed at my excitement.

I jumped and spun around in dizzying circles. "I'm gonna go get that rainbow, Papau.... I wanna touch it."

"Is that right?"

"Yes! Yes!" I charged down the hill, stumbling, giddy and breathless at the thought of hauling my rainbow home. I tumbled through the weeds, toppled into an occasional mud puddle, and tore through thorn bushes—all the while trying to figure out how I could convince my mom to let me keep the rainbow.

I ran faster and faster, squealing every time it seemed just within reach. But when my heart began to pound, my lungs burn for air, I realized the rainbow was eluding me. The airy bands or color floated weightlessly across the valley, always just ahead. I was chasing a rainbow, chasing something that wasn't meant for me.

I suddenly stopped running, black curls tumbling over my flushed face, and turned to see that Papau had followed me.

"It got away, Papau." My mouth began to quiver and a sob rose in my throat.

"Right over there it is, Lora," he said, picking me up.

"I know, but it's on the other side of the fence." I touched his stubbled cheek for emphasis, and wrapped my arms around his neck. "I wanted to keep it."

"Well, I reckon it might belong to someone else." He lowered me gently to the ground.

"You think so, Papau?" I yanked on his overalls, trying to get him to look down.

"I do believe so, little girl." He smiled and took my soft hand in his calloused one, and we walked toward the tiny white square at the bottom of the valley.

Feeling better, I fell in stride. "Can I wear your hat?"

He grinned, blue eyes twinkling as he put his hat on my head. "Why? You gonna drive my tractor, too?"

I nodded, giggling as the hat slipped down over my eyes. We were almost home when I turned around once more, peering out from under the huge rim at the now fading rainbow. After one last glance, I turned back around, hugging Papau's leg tightly. "Maybe someone else needs it more, Papau." I thought about it a little. "Yeah, maybe someone else needs it more."

Fifteen years and hundreds of morning walks later, as I ride through rush-hour traffic, I remember my rainbow-chasing days—this time, with tears. We are all crying—my mom, brother, and I. Papau is dying. His nurse has told us by phone that we won't get there in time, that even if we could, he wouldn't know we were there. And I feel as though my world is falling apart.

My mother races through the thick traffic, braving the onslaught of honking horns, red lights, and a severe downpour of rain. She drives methodically, mechanically, keeping time with the wipers swishing rhythmically over the window, not allowing herself to think of anything but getting to her father.

Silently, I pray. I pray that we will make it in time, pleading with God to let me see Papau once more, so I can talk to him again, so I can tell him goodbye, that he'll see Jesus soon, that I will miss him. That I love him.

Staring blankly out my window at the gray sheets of rain, I begin to doubt. All I can think of is, *What will I do if I don't see him? What will I do?* As I feel fear nipping at my heart, I pray desperately, begging God for just one more time with my gentle friend.

I ask for a rainbow.

My heart is empty, and words seem hollow now. So I simply ask for a rainbow.

I'm not sure why, but when I can only see gray outside the window and inside my heart, I realize only a rainbow will do. Only a brilliant stroke of color painted by God's very hand across the black canvas of sky will calm my heart. I am chasing rainbows again.

Hours pass, however, and I scan the darkening horizon for a triumph of color, grasping for something that assures me God hears my cry. But I find nothing. Absolutely nothing.

For a while, I pray angrily, asking God why he couldn't grant me this one tiny request, this one spark of assurance. He sent Noah one, didn't he? God gave Noah a sign that he would never leave him or forsake him, that he was always there. Well, where is God now?

As ashen twilight fades into black night, the soothing hum of the car lulls me to sleep. I sleep for hours until I hear a door slamming, feel my mother shaking me awake. Her face is drawn and pale. We enter the hospital, nauseated by the clinical smell and by the stark whiteness I now associate with pain and death, but I keep trudging along numbly.

Nurses and doctors buzz by, calling out orders. Patients are wheeled by on carts. But sights and sounds blend into one dull drone and I focus on one open door at the end of the hallway.

My aunt rushes down the hall to meet us, answering our unspoken question. "He's still alive, but he doesn't know anything that's going on." We all hug each other grateful for at least that. We walk together toward Papau's room.

But then she turns and stops, her face suddenly aglow. "Betty, De'Lara, the strangest thing happened a few hours ago, when Papau was conscious. He was in a lot of pain, having trouble breathing." She leaned against the wall, searching for words. "He seemed restless. We had a terrible storm here and all the rain and clouds were depressing him, I think. But suddenly, from out of nowhere, this gorgeous rainbow appeared. It just seemed to pour into the room through the window. And I could tell it took Papau's mind off his pain for a while, it soothed him somehow and he finally fell asleep. It was almost like it came straight from heaven. Absolutely unreal. I haven't ever seen anything like it in my life."

I have. Oh, I have. About fifteen years ago. And although I enter the room now and see my Papau wrapped in a tangle of tubes, fighting for every breath, I have a certain peace about the situation. About the rainbow I thought I didn't get. God was in control and he knew someone just needed it more.

Although the nurses and doctors assured us he would not last through the night, Papau was better the next day. God allowed me to spend that entire Saturday with him—a wonderful Saturday of recalling memories we had all made together. We laughed and teased, although I occasionally left the room and cried, feeling as though my life would surely end with his. But I always came back a few minutes later to laugh again.

When it was time to leave, I wrapped my arms around his neck as I had done for twenty years, telling him how much I loved him. Weakly, he hugged me back and whispered hoarsely, "I do you too, Lora." That was the quiet way he had always expressed his love. I held onto him for a long time, somehow knowing this would be our last embrace this side of heaven.

Papau died a week later.

It has been eight months since my gentle friend died, and although I still feel a stab of grief when I remember all the times we spent together— the morning walks, the late-night checker games, the joke-telling sessions that could last for hours at a time. When my heart is overcast and gray from missing him, I can see the wonder in his eyes when he saw a rainbow from heaven, and I realize that God is always there.

I know I will see Papau some day and we will take long morning walks and chase shimmering rainbows again. And this time, considering where we'll be, I just bet we'll catch one.

Success is not to be pursued,
It is to be attracted by the person you become.

—*Author unknown*

Grandma's Garden

Lynnette Curtis

Each year, my Grandmother Inez planted tulips in her flower garden and looked forward to their springtime beauty with childlike anticipation. Under her loving guardianship, they sprang up each April faithfully, and she was never disappointed. But she said the real flowers that decorated her life were her grandchildren.

I, for one, was not going to play along.

I was sent to stay with my grandmother when I was sixteen years old. My parents lived overseas and I was a very troubled young woman, full of false wisdom and anger at them for their inability to cope with or understand me. An unhappy, disrespectful teenager, I was ready to drop out of school.

Grandma was a tiny woman, towered over by her own children and their not-yet-grown offspring, and she possessed a classic, old-fashioned prettiness. Her hair was dark and elegantly styled, and her eyes were of the clearest blue, vibrant, and glittering with energy and intensity. She was ruled by an extraordinary loyalty to family, and she loved as profoundly and sincerely as a child. Still, I thought my grandmother would be easier to ignore than my parents.

I moved into her humble farmhouse silently, skulking about with my head hung low and eyes downcast like an abused pet. I had given up on others, instead cocooning myself within a hard shell of apathy. I refused to allow another soul admittance to my private world because my greatest fear was that someone would discover my secret vulnerabilities. I was convinced life was a bitter struggle better fought on one's own.

I expected nothing from grandmother but to be left alone, and planned to accept nothing less. She, however, did not give up so easily.

School began and I attended classes occasionally, spending the rest of my days in my pajamas, staring dully at the television set in my bedroom. Not taking the hint, Grandma burst through my door each morning like an unwelcome ray of sunshine.

"Good morning!" she'd sing, cheerfully raising the blinds from my window. I pulled my blanket over my head and ignored her.

When I did stray from my bedroom, I was barraged with a string of well-meant questions from her regarding my health, my thoughts and my views on the world in general. I answered in mumbled monosyllables, but somehow she was not discouraged. In fact, she acted as if my meaningless grunts fascinated her; she listened with as much solemnity and interest as if we were engaged in an intense conversation in which I had just revealed an intimate secret. On those rare occasions when I happened to offer more than a one-word response, she would clap her hands together joyously and smile hugely, as if I had presented her with a great gift.

At first, I wondered if she just didn't get it. However, though she wasn't an educated woman, I sensed she had the simple common-sense smarts that come from natural intelligence. Married at age thirteen during the Great Depression, she learned what she needed to know about life by raising five children through difficult economic times, cooking in other people's restaurants, and eventually running a restaurant of her own.

So I shouldn't have been surprised when she insisted I learn to make bread. I was such a failure at kneading that Grandma would take over at that stage of the process. However, she wouldn't allow me to leave the kitchen until the bread was set out to rise. It was during those times, when her attention was focused away from me and I stared at the flower garden outside the window of the kitchen, that I first began to talk to her. She listened with such eagerness that I was sometimes embarrassed.

Slowly, as I realized my grandmother's interest in me did not wear off with the novelty of my presence, I opened up to her more and more. I began to secretly yet fervently look forward to our talks.

When the words finally came to me, they would not stop. I began attending school regularly, and rushed home each afternoon to find her sitting in her usual chair, smiling and waiting to hear a detailed account of the minutes of my day.

One day in my junior year, I hurried through the door to Grandma's side and announced, "I was named editor of the high school newspaper!"

She gasped and clapped her hands over her mouth. More moved than I could ever be, she seized both my hands in hers and squeezed them, fiercely. I looked into her eyes, which were sparkling like mad. She said, "I like you so much, and I am very proud of you!"

Her words hit me with such force that I couldn't respond. Those words did more for me than a thousand "I love you's." I knew her love was unconditional, but her friendship and pride were things to earn. To receive them both from this incredible woman made me begin to wonder whether there was, in fact, something likable and worthy within myself. She awakened in me a desire to discover my own potential, and a reason to allow others to know my vulnerabilities.

On that day, I decided to try to live as she did—with energy and intensity. I was suddenly flushed with an appetite to explore the world, my mind, and the hearts of others, to love as freely and unconditionally as she had. And I realized that I loved her—not because she was my grandmother, but because she was a beautiful individual who had taught me what she knew about caring for herself and others.

My grandmother passed away in the springtime, nearly two years after I came to live with her, and two months before I graduated from high school.

She died encircled by her children and grandchildren, who held hands and remembered a life filled with love and happiness. Before she left this world, each of us leaned over her bed, with moist eyes and faces, and kissed her tenderly. As my turn came, I kissed her gently on the cheek, took her hand and whispered, "I like you so much, Grandma, and I am very proud of you!"

Now, as I prepare to graduate from college, I often think of my grandmother's words, and hope she would still feel proud of me. I marvel at the kindness and patience with which she helped me emerge from a difficult childhood to a young womanhood filled with peace. I picture her in the springtime, as the tulips in her garden, and we, her offspring, still bloom with an enthusiasm equaled only by her own. And I continue to work to make sure she will never be disappointed.

Sunshine

Those who bring sunshine to the lives of others
cannot keep it from themselves.

—Alexander Chalmbers

From Chicago, With Love

MARVIN J. WOLF
CONDENSED FROM *CHICAGO TRIBUNE MAGAZINE*

When I was nine, I needed to earn money, so I asked Mr. Miceli, the Herald-American's man in my Chicago neighborhood, about an after-school paper route. He said if I had a bicycle, he'd give me a route.

My dad was working four jobs then. He built neon signs in a sheet-metal shop during the day, delivered flowers until eight in the evening, drove a cab till midnight, and on weekends sold insurance door to door. He bought me a used bike, but right after that he was hospitalized with pneumonia and couldn't teach me how to ride. Mr. Miceli, on the other hand, hadn't asked to see me ride. He merely asked to see the bike. So I walked it down to his garage, showed it to him, and got the job.

At first, I slung my delivery sack filled with rolled papers over the handlebars and walked my bike down the sidewalks. But pushing a bike with a load of paper was awkward. After a few days I left the bike at home and borrowed Moms two wheeled steel-mesh shopping cart.

Delivering papers from a bike is tricky. You get one chance to throw each paper, and if it misses the porch or stoop, too bad. But I left Mom's cart at the sidewalk and carried each paper to its proper destination. If that was a second-floor porch, and I missed the first throw, I retrieved the paper and threw again. On Sundays, when the papers were big and heavy, I carried each one up the stairs. If it was raining, I put my papers inside the screen doors or, at apartment buildings, in the entrance halls. In rain or snow I put Dad's old raincoat over the cart to keep the papers dry.

It took me longer to make my deliveries by cart than if I were on a bike, but I didn't mind. I got to meet everyone in the neighborhood—working-class people of Italian, German, or Polish descent who were invariably kind to me. If I saw something interesting while walking my route, such as a dog with puppies or a rainbow of oil on wet asphalt, I could stop to watch for a while.

When Dad returned from the hospital, he resumed his day job, but he was too weak to work the others and had to give them up. Now we needed every dime we could raise to pay bills, so we sold my bike. Since I still didn't know how to ride it, I didn't object.

Mr. Miceli must have known I wasn't using a bike, but he said nothing about it to me. In fact, he rarely spoke to any of us boys, unless it was to give us a hard time for missing a customer or leaving a paper in a puddle.

In eight months I built my route from thirty-six subscribers to fifty-nine, mostly because customers sent me to their neighbors, who said they wanted to take the paper. Sometimes people stopped me on the street to tell me to add them to my list.

I earned a penny a paper, Monday through Saturday, and a nickel a paper on Sundays. I collected every Thursday evening, and since most customers gave me a nickel or a dime extra, soon I was making almost as much in tips as I got in pay from Mr. Miceli. That was good, because Dad still couldn't work much and I had to give most of my wages to Mom.

On the Thursday evening before Christmas 1951, I rang my first customer's doorbell. Even though the lights were on nobody answered the door so I went on to the next house. No answer. The same thing happened at the next family's house and the one after that. Soon I had knocked and rung at most of my subscribers' doors, but not one person appeared to be home.

I was very worried; I had to pay for my papers every Friday. And while it was almost Christmas I'd never thought everyone would be out shopping.

So I was very happy when going up the walkway to the Gordons' house, I heard music and voices. I rang the bell. Instantly the door was flung open, and Mr. Gordon all but dragged me inside.

Jammed into his living room were almost all my fifty-nine subscribers. In the middle of the room was a brand-new Schwinn bicycle. It was candy-apple red, and it had a generator-powered headlight and a bell. A canvas bag bulging with colorful envelopes hung from the handlebars.

"This is for you," Mrs. Gordon said. "We all chipped in."

The envelopes held Christmas cards, along with the weekly subscription fees. Most also included a generous tip. I was dumbstruck. I didn't know what to say. Finally, one of the women called for quiet and gently led me to the center of the room. "You are the best paperboy we've ever had," she said. "There's never been a day when a paper was missing or late, never a day when it got wet. We've all seen you out there in the rain and snow with that little shopping cart. And so we thought you ought to have a bicycle."

All I could say was "thank you." I said it over and over.

When I got home, I counted more than $100 in tips—a windfall that made me a family hero and brought our household a wonderful holiday season.

My subscribers must have called Mr. Miceli, because when I got to his garage the next day to pick up my papers, he was waiting outside. "Bring your bike tomorrow at ten and I'll teach you how to ride," he said, and I did.

When I had begun to feel comfortable on the bike, Mr. Miceli asked me to deliver a second route, forty-two papers. Delivering both routes from my new bike went faster than delivering one from the shopping cart.

But when it rained, I got off my bike to carry every paper to a dry haven. And if I missed a throw to a high porch, I stopped, put down the kickstand and threw again.

I joined the Army after high school and gave away my Schwinn to my younger brother Ted. I can't recall what became of it. But my subscribers gave me another gift—a shining lesson about taking pride in even the humblest work, a Christmas present I try to use as often as I remember the kind Chicagoans who gave it to me.

Óne Phóne Call

If you were going to die soon and had
only one phone call you could make,
who would you call and what would you say?
And why are you waiting?

—Stephen Levine

Picking Up the Pieces

JENNIFER LEIGH YOUNGS
FROM *TASTE BERRIES FOR TEENS*

When I was in ninth grade, a boy I was sure I was in love with started dating my best friend. Just like that. One day he was walking me to my locker; and the next day, he was walking my very best friend to her locker. "We're not going together anymore!" he announced, and in the same breath added, "I'm going with Tammy now."

I didn't know how to "fix it." I didn't know what to think or how to feel. Should I be mad at him? Angry with my best friend? How should I explain it to my friends?

I was clear about one thing: I hurt all over. No one, not even my friends or brothers or sisters or parents really knew how deeply I was hurting. I didn't want to go to school. I didn't want to go to soccer practice. I didn't want to do anything. I just wanted to be alone. I didn't want to talk with anyone about it—certainly not my parents.

Not that it stopped them from asking. Noting that I was upset at just about everyone and everything, Mom asked, "Would you like to talk about what's bothering you?"

"No!" I cried.

"Talking can make it better," Mom remined me.

"It's just about my stupid best friend. I'll be okay," I said, hoping I didn't have to explain anymore.

She didn't ask again, no doubt assuming that I'd tell her about it when I was ready. In the meantime, my parents were extra kind and tried to give me the space I needed; like a couple of times they allowed me to eat dinner in my room rather than coming to the dinner table.

After about a week or so of my still being tearful, my mother stepped up her inspection of the issue. "I can see you are suffering over this," she said. "I think we should talk about it."

"Oh, Mom," I cried. "It hurts too much to talk about it!"

"Yes, honey," she soothed, "I can see that you are hurting."

"Why does it hurt so much?" I asked.

"Pain is God's way of saying your heart is broken."

"I don't need God to tell me my heart is broken," I cried. "I just need him to fix it."

"Well," my mother counseled tenderly, "better give him all the pieces. God can't fix your broken heart if you don't give all the pieces to him."

I'll always remember those beautiful words: "God can't fix a broken heart if you don't give him all the pieces."

The Winner

Sharon Jaynes

t was the first swim meet of the year for our newly formed Middle School Aquatics team. The atmosphere on the three hour bus ride was electric with anticipation as the band of forty-eight adolescents thought of nothing but victory. However, the electricity turned into shock as our minnows filed off the bus and stared in disbelief at their muscle clad Greek-god-like opponents.

The coach checked the schedule. "Surely there's been a mistake," he thought. But the schedule only confirmed that, yes, this was the right place and the right time.

The two teams formed a line on the side of the pool. Whistles blew, races were begun, and races were lost. Halfway through the meet, Coach Huey realized that he had no participants for one of the events.

"Okay team, who wants to swim the five-hundred-yard free style?" the coach asked.

Several hands shot up, including Justin Rigsbee's. "I'll race, Coach!"

The coach looked down at the freckle faced youth and said, "Justin, this race is twenty lengths of the pool. I've only seen you swim eight."

"Oh, I can do it, Coach. Let me try. What's twelve more laps?"

Coach Huey reluctantly conceded. "After all," he thought, "it's not the winning but the trying that builds character."

The whistle blew and the opponents torpedoed through the water and finished the race in a mere four minutes and fifty seconds. The winners gathered on the sidelines to socialize while our group struggled to finish. After four more long minutes, the last exhausted members of our team emerged from the water. The last except for Justin.

Justin was stealing breaths as his hands slapped against the water and pushed it aside to propel his thin body forward. It appeared that he would go under at any minute, yet something seemed to keep pushing him onward.

"Why doesn't the coach stop this child?" the parents whispered among themselves. "He looks like he's about to drown and the race was won four minutes ago."

But what the parents did not realize was that the real race, the race of a boy becoming a man, was just beginning.

The coach walked over to the young swimmer, knelt down and quietly spoke.

Relieved parents thought, *Oh, he's finally going to pull that boy out before he kills himself.*

But to their surprise, the coach rose from the concrete, stepped back from the pool's edge, and the young man continued to swim.

One teammate, inspired by his brave friend, went to the side of the pool and walked the lane as Justin pressed on. "Come on, Justin, you can do it! You can do it! Keep going! Don't give up!"

He was joined by another, then another, until the entire team was walking the length of the pool rooting for and encouraging their fellow swimmer to finish the race set before him.

The opposing team saw what was happening and joined the chant. The students' contagious chorus sent a chill through the room and soon the once concerned parents were on their feet cheering, shouting, and praying. The room was pulsating with energy and excitement as teammates and opponents alike pumped courage into one small swimmer.

Twelve long minutes after the starting whistle had blown, an exhausted, but smiling, Justin Rigsbee swam his final lap and pulled himself out of the pool. The crowd had applauded the first swimmer as he crossed the line in first place. But the standing ovation they gave Justin that day was proof that the greater victory was his, just for finishing the race.

The Red Chevy

BOB CARLISLE
FROM *SONS: A FATHER'S LOVE*

y father loved cars. He tuned them up, rubbed them down, and knew every sound and smell and idiosyncrasy of every car he owned. He was also very picky about who drove his cars. So when I got my driver's license at sixteen, I was a little worried about the responsibility of leaving home in one of his beloved vehicles. He had a beautiful red Chevy pickup, a big white Suburban, and a Mustang convertible with a hot V-8 engine. Every one of them was in prime condition. He also had a short temper and very little patience with carelessness, especially if his kids happened to be the careless ones.

One afternoon he sent me to town in the Chevy truck with the assignment of bringing back a list of things he needed for some odd jobs around the house. It hadn't been long since I'd gotten my license, so it was still a novelty to be seen driving around, and Dad's red pickup was a good truck to be seen in. I carefully maneuvered my way toward downtown, watching carefully at each light, trying to drive as defensively as he'd always told me to do. The thought of a collision in one of Dad's cars was

173

enough to make me the safest driver in town. I didn't even want to think about it.

I was heading through a green light and was in the middle of a main downtown intersection when an elderly man, who somehow hadn't seen the red light, plowed into the passenger side of the Chevy. I slammed on the brakes, hit a slick spot in the road, and spun into a curb; the pickup rolled over onto its side.

I was dazed at first, and my face was bleeding from a couple of glass cuts, but the seat belt had kept me from serious injury. I was vaguely concerned about the danger of fire, but the engine had died, and before long I heard the sound of sirens. I had just begun to wonder how much longer I'd be trapped inside when a couple of firemen helped me get out, and soon I was sitting on the curb, my aching head in my hands, my face and shirt dripping with blood.

That's when I got a good look at Dad's red pickup. It was scraped and dented and crushed, and I was surprised that I had walked away from it in one piece. And by then I was sort of wishing I hadn't, because it suddenly dawned on me that I would soon have to face Dad with some very bad news about one of his pride-and-joy cars.

We lived in a small town, and several people who saw the accident knew me. Someone must have called Dad right away, because it wasn't long after I was rescued from the wreck that he came running up to me. I closed my eyes, not wanting to see his face.

"Dad, I'm so sorry—"

"Terry, are you all right?" Dad's voice didn't sound at all like I thought it would. When I looked up, he was on his knees next to me on the curb, his hands gently lifting my cut face and studying my wounds. "Are you in a lot of pain?"

"I'm okay. I'm really sorry about your truck."

"Forget the truck, Terry. The truck's a piece of machinery. I'm concerned about you, not the truck. Can you get up? Can you walk? I'll drive you to the hospital unless you think you need an ambulance."

I shook my head. "I don't need an ambulance. I'm fine."

Dad carefully put his hands under my arms and lifted me to my feet.

I looked up at him uncertainly and was amazed to see that his face was a study in compassion and concern. "Can you make it?" he asked, and his voice sounded scared.

"I'm fine, Dad. Really. Why don't we just go home? I don't need to go to the hospital."

We compromised and went to the family doctor, who cleaned up my wounds, bandaged me, and sent me on my way. I don't recall when the truck got towed, what I did for the rest of that night, or how long I was laid up. All I know is that for the first time in my life, I understood that my father loved me. I hadn't realized it before, but Dad loved me more than his truck, more than any of his cars, more than I could have possibly imagined.

Since that day we've had our ups and downs, and I've disappointed him enough to make him mad, but one thing remains unchanging. Dad loved me then, he loves me now, and he'll love me for the rest of my life.

Tough Teacher

RENIE PARSONS

My mother was a teacher from the old-school. She believed that education was essential to making a good life. She believed that discipline was an important part of education. Every freshman in our small town was in her freshman English class. She was a tough teacher. She believed she had to be. She believed everyone should be able to read the newspaper and that everyone could learn proper spelling and grammar. Many of her students disagreed.

I was aware that she was not a popular teacher. Even so, I held a certain admiration for her. My mother was raised on a farm her daddy never owned. He rented the land to grow cotton. The thirteen children were expected to work picking cotton and growing most of the food they ate. It was back-breaking work which they did without complaint.

One of my mother's favorite sayings was, "That which does not kill you will make you strong." I knew she was very strong and "that which did not kill" her had made her so strong.

I remember one school day when my junior-high friends and I raced over to the local hamburger joint for a quick lunch. The place was crowded with students, most of whom were in high school. There was one boy in particular who was handsome beyond belief. I knew who he was but would have died before I did anything to attract attention from him. I just wanted to get close enough to say that I had been right there by him at lunch.

He was shouting to a friend above the noise of the crowd. I just had to know what he was saying. This would be gossip on the highest level. I kept moving in, closer and closer, until I was right by his side. I turned to give a girlfriend that all-knowing look of having accomplished my mission.

His voice became clearer and clearer until I could actually hear his words. The words were unkind words. Language that I had not been exposed to at age thirteen. Harsh words. Someone had really made him angry. I listened until I was able to catch enough of the conversation to realize that it was my mother he was talking about.

Although I too was often a recipient of my mother's overzealous discipline, I knew she did not deserve this boy's bitter ranting. I tapped his arm and said simply, "That's my mother you're talking about."

He turned toward me, and I knew instantly that I could have asked for the world, and he would have given it. Fear was written in a dark red blush straight across his face. It was a moment of power that silenced the roar of the lunch crowd. He was terrified that I would tell my mother what I had heard. He began pleading and begging for my silence. The excuses mounted up and up as I stood staring at him. "You don't understand. You don't know what she'll do to me. I have to get an A in this class. I was just angry. I didn't mean what I said. You can't tell her. She'll kill me! Please. Please. Please."

I said nothing. I turned and walked away. I understood his fear. I wouldn't tell her. How can you tell your mother something like that?

I often felt like my mother was a tyrant after that. I knew she was a good teacher in that she expected her students to learn in her class. But I still believed that much of what that boy had said must be true.

A couple of years later, I became a student in her English class. It was a tough year. I spent most of it in the back of the room. At a table with a chair. By myself. Because I talked too much in class.

Later that year, my mother and I were leaving the dime store when a young man stopped us at the sidewalk. He was dressed in a Navy uniform and looked quite snappy propped against the parking meter. I vaguely remembered him as a graduate from our high school a year or so before.

I eavesdropped on their conversation. It began like this: "Mrs. McGuire, I owe you an apology. I was a difficult student when I had you for English." She nodded in recognition of the truth of his statement. "All I wanted to do was play football. But you wouldn't just pass me through. I hated you for that. But you made me learn. You made me learn grammar and spelling. I wasn't good at either one, but I worked hard so I could make the grades for football. Still only made a C in your class."

My mother half-smiled in remembrance.

"I just wanted you to know, I did learn a lot from you. After high school, I joined the Navy to avoid getting drafted into the Army. They made me a secretary because I was the only one in my outfit who could spell and use proper grammar. Mrs. McGuire, almost all the other boys were sent to Vietnam. A lot of them didn't come home. I'm alive today because of you. Thank you for making me learn. I apologize for being so difficult."

My mother thanked him and admonished him to continue learning.

I was astonished. My mother had saved someone's life. I teared up as I asked her about the young man. In her usual way, she told me how silly I was to cry. After all, she reminded me, crying never accomplished anything. As we got in the car to drive home, I glanced over to look at my mother's face. She casually brushed away a single tear forming at the corner of her eye.

I never thought of her as a tyrant again.

"LOOK AT IT THIS WAY... THE ODDS OF THAT EVER HAPPENING AGAIN ARE ALMOST IMPOSSIBLE!"

All Changes Begin With You

SEAN COVEY
FROM THE 7 HABITS OF HIGHLY EFFECTIVE TEENS

W hat's wrong with you? You're disappointing me. Where's the Sean I once knew in high school?" Coach glared at me. "Do you even want to be out there?"

I was shocked. "Yes, of course."

"Oh, give me a break. You're just going through the motions and your heart's not in it. You better get your act together or the younger quarterbacks will pass you by and you'll never play here."

It was my sophomore year at Brigham Young University (BYU) during preseason football camp. Coming out of high school, I was recruited by several colleges but chose BYU because they had a tradition of producing all-American quarterbacks like Jim McMahon and Steve Young, both of whom went on to the pros and led their teams to Super Bowl victories. Although I was the third-string quarterback at the time, I wanted to be the next all-American!

When Coach told me that I was "stinkin' up the field," it came as a cold, hard slap in the face. The thing that really bugged me was that he was right. Even though I was spending long hours practicing, I wasn't truly committed. I was holding back and knew it.

I had a hard decision to make—I had to either quit football or triple my commitment. Over the next several weeks, I waged a war inside my head and came face-to-face with many fears and self-doubts. Did I have what it took to be the starting quarterback? Could I handle the pressure? Was I big enough? It soon became clear to me that I was scared, scared of competing, scared of being in the limelight, scared of trying and perhaps failing. And all these fears were holding me back from giving it my all.

I read a great quote by Arnold Bennett that describes what I finally decided to do about my dilemma. He wrote, "The real tragedy is the tragedy of the man who never in his life braces himself for his one supreme effort—he never stretches to his full capacity, never stands up to his full stature."

Having never enjoyed tragedy, I decided to brace myself for one supreme effort. So I committed to give it my all. I decided to stop holding back and lay it all on the line. I didn't know if I would ever get a chance to be first string, but if I didn't, at least I was going to strike out swinging.

No one heard me say, "I commit." There was no applause. It was simply a private battle I fought and won inside my own mind over a period of several weeks.

Once I committed myself, everything changed. I began taking chances and making big improvements on the field. My heart was in it. And the coaches took notice.

As the season began and the games rolled by one by one, I sat on the bench. Although frustrated, I kept working hard and kept improving.

Midseason featured the big game of the year. We were to play national ranked Air Force on ESPN, in front of 65,000 fans. A week before the game, Coach called me into his office and told me that I would be the starting quarterback. Gulp! Needless to say, that was the longest week of my life.

Game day finally arrived. At kickoff my mouth was so dry I could barely talk. But after a few minutes I settled down and led our team to victory. I was even named the ESPN Player of the Game. Afterward, lots of people congratulated me on the victory and my performance. That was nice. But they didn't really understand.

They didn't know the real story. They thought that victory had taken place on the field that day in the public eye. I knew it happened months before in the privacy of my own head, when I decided to face my fears, to stop holding back, and to brace myself for one supreme effort. Beating Air Force was a much easier challenge than overcoming myself. Private victories always come before public victories. As the saying goes, "We have met the enemy and he is us."

A Basket of Love

CHRIS A. WOLFF

In a gymnasium in Southern California some fifteen years ago, two junior varsity girls' basketball teams faced off in a contest that meant nothing more to most than a hash mark on either side of a win/lose column. To most who were there the memory of that game has either faded or completely disappeared. But as a participant in that game, I tell you it is a memory that is permanently etched in my heart and mind.

We were playing the toughest team in our high school league. They were intimidating in size, skill, and number. We, on the other hand, were small, inexperienced, and shaking in our little basketball shoes. After assessing our chances of a victory, we set for ourselves a reasonable and practical goal: Try not to get killed!

As the game got underway we found ourselves in an unexpected position. We were losing all right, but only by a few points. Throughout the second quarter we managed to tie the score several times. After halftime the lead changed hands frequently. The outcome of the game was entirely up in the air. We were no longer the underdogs. In fact, we had a good chance of beating the best team in our league.

As the clock wound down to the final seconds of the fourth quarter, we were behind by just one point. We had nineteen seconds left to score the winning basket. As the other team brought the ball in bounds and headed toward their basket I moved up to the half-court line to meet my opponent. With the distance between us closing, I heard a voice in my head say, *I'm going to steal this ball from her!* But I had no more time to think, I could only react. My opponent was only inches away. So, I reached out with my right hand and lunged toward the ball. Much to the surprise of both of us, the ball went from her hand into mine. I now had not only the ball, but the fate of the game, resting in my hands.

I ran toward our basket and when I arrived, I lifted the ball as high as I could stretch. The ball landed delicately on the rim. The adrenaline in my body carried me right off the court and I watched the ball through the back of the glass backboard. It traveled around the rim once, then a second time, and finally a third time. The third time around, the ball fell... right off the front of the rim and into the hands of the girl from whom I had stolen it. *I had missed the basket!* I stood there in shock. A few seconds later, I heard the buzzer sound. The game was over and we had lost by one point.

I was still a bit dazed as I made my way to the bench. When I saw my teammates I began to cry. I had let them down. I had lost the game for us. But when I saw my coach I was even more overwhelmed with sadness and embarrassment. I felt so ashamed. I didn't want her to look at me. I wanted to crawl into a hole and disappear. I thought to myself, "How could I have let her down?"

My coach was one of the most important people in my life. She was my hero. She was the first person in my life that I looked up to and admired. I loved her not only for the personal qualities that I saw in her and desired for myself, but also because I knew she saw something special in me. As a fourteen-year-old skinny little girl with glasses, I didn't think anyone could possibly see anything special in me. But my coach did.

After things settled down a bit, I went to the rest room to regain my composure. As I walked out of the gym, I purposely avoided my coach. I was sure that the "special" piece inside of me that she had seen and loved had vanished. I was a loser! Everyone in that gym was a witness to that fact. I couldn't hide it. The truth about me had been revealed: I was nothing special. I was a failure. Although I knew I had to face her eventually, I wanted to delay it as long as possible. I wanted to prepare myself for the moment I would see in her eyes that I was no longer "special."

After several minutes, I left the rest room. In the hallway, I took one last deep breath, squared my shoulders and prepared as best I could to face all those who had just witnessed my failure. With my first step toward the double doors, I saw one of them begin to open. I froze in my tracks and held my breath. As the door eased open I saw my coach.

My immediate reaction was to look for a place to hide. But in the small hallway there was nowhere to go. For a moment we stood facing each other and then slowly walked toward each other. As I came within inches of her, I spoke only two words, "I'm sorry." They came out in a whisper, as again I was overwhelmed with emotion. Her six-foot figure loomed over me and her lanky arms embraced me. She tilted her head close to mine and said, "I wouldn't trade you for anyone."

I repeated her words to myself, "I wouldn't trade you for anyone." It took a few seconds for me to grasp that concept. With six words, my coach had filled me with an unearned, overflowing, tremendously powerful feeling of love. It was the only thing she said to me that night, and it was more than enough.

Good Times

Things I've Learned Lately...

Midnight laughing cleanses you,
Little girls need to feel pretty,
Having fun with someone opens the door to friendship,
And Christmas is love.

We Could Have Danced All Night

GUY RICE DOUD
FROM *MOLDER OF DREAMS*

As adviser to our high school student council I worked with the leadership to encourage projects that involved student service. I was impressed with my students' enthusiasm for helping with local canned-food drives and other events to aid charity.

Our "Adopt-a-Grandparent" program had been rewarding for the students who had been involved. They had grown as people by discovering the worth of others. I believe that the true leader is the true servant, and I tried to convey that message to my students. But it never got through to them as clearly as it did the night of the prom.

Tom Rosenberger had given me a call. A friend, and one of the local elementary principals, Tom had heard of an idea at a conference he had attended and called to share the idea with me. I fell in love with it and soon shared it with my student council.

"Mr. President?" I asked.

Mike, the president of the student council, acknowledged me. "Yes, Mr. Doud?"

I started gradually. "I've been thinking of an idea, and I want to bounce it off everyone."

"What's the idea?" asked Mike.

"I think we should host a prom." I said.

"We already have a prom!" answered about thirty students all at once, who seemed to wonder if I had lost my mind. They knew that organizing the prom was the responsibility of the junior class cabinet.

"Oh, I don't mean a prom for eleventh and twelfth graders," I said.

"We're not going to include sophomores!" said one senior boy.

"No. I want to have a prom for senior—" but they didn't let me finish.

"Seniors can already go to the prom," Mike answered, wondering what had gone wrong with his adviser.

"No, for senior citizens. People fifty-five years of age and over. Let's hold a prom for them."

"Why would we want to do that?" asked Mike.

"Let's take the money we've earned this year," I said, "and let's give it back to the community in the form of a gift. That gift will be a prom. We'll invite all senior citizens to come. We'll decorate the gym, hire an orchestra, have corsages for the ladies...." I was beginning to show some real excitement.

"If we spent money doing that, does that mean we wouldn't take our usual spring trip?" asked one girl, putting down the mirror she held in her hand.

"We would spend as much of the money as necessary to make this a most special evening for the senior citizens. The orchestra we hire will play the big band sounds of the twenties and thirties and other dance music. I've already contacted an orchestra, and I've talked with our principal, who thinks it's a great idea. I told him that I thought you guys would think it's a great idea, too." I can be pretty persuasive sometimes.

After much discussion, the council voted to form a committee to plan the senior citizen prom. In the weeks to follow, I watched my students become excited about the prom. Some of the young men in the council decided to order tuxedos so they would look nice as hosts. The girls planned to wear their long dresses to serve as hostesses.

All of Brainerd got excited the week before the prom. Paul Harvey began page two of this national daily broadcast his way: "In Brainerd, Minnesota, the student council is planning a prom...for senior citizens. That's right! A prom...for senior citizens. The Brainerd students are going to provide an orchestra, corsages, valet parking, free hors d'oeuvres and...they are also going to do the chaperoning!"

I had been somewhat concerned about the lack of advertising. My students had contacted the senior citizen centers in the area and had sent out invitations, but when I heard it announced by Paul Harvey, my fears of poor publicity died.

The night of the prom finally arrived. The students had decorated our gym more beautifully than I had ever seen it. It was like the gym I had seen in my dreams when I had been in high school. The floral department at the vocational school had donated corsages, some of the local banks provided the hors d'oeuvres, the bus company that contracts with the school district provided free transportation to any senior citizen needing it. My students had tried to cover all the bases. We sat back to wait and see how many seniors would attend. The prom was to begin at six-thirty. At four o'clock, they started to come!

One of the first to arrive was an older lady with a cane. She stopped inside the door and looked around.

"Oh," she said, "so this is the new high school."

I didn't remind her that the high school was more than fifteen years old.

"I've never been in here before," she said.

Mark Dinham, one of the main organizers of the prom, grabbed a corsage and asked her if he could pin it on her. She readily agreed.

"The prom doesn't begin until six-thirty," Mark said.

"I'll wait," she said. "I want to get a good seat."

"I hope you'll do some dancing!" I said.

"I'll dance if you dance with me!" she replied as Mark finished pinning her corsage.

He turned a bit red. "Sure, I'll dance with you, but I've got to go home and change clothes," he said.

A few moments later, a couple walked up to the table. "Is this where the prom is being held?" they asked.

"That's right," I said.

I could hardly believe what they had to say: "We're from Oregon, and we're on our way to Wisconsin. We heard it on Paul Harvey yesterday, so we looked up Brainerd on the map and decided to go a little out of our way so we could come to your prom. Are we welcome?"

And people kept coming. By 6:30 when the prom began, more than five hundred senior citizens packed the transformed gymnasium.

But we had developed one major problem. Mike was the first to call it to my attention. I had noticed him dancing with one lady after another. He wasn't able to take a break.

"Mr. Doud," he said, "we have a serious male shortage here."

"What are you going to do about it, Mike?" I asked.

"I know where some of the hockey team is tonight, and I think I could call them and tell them to go home and get their suits on and get over here."

"Good plan," I said.

Soon some of Mike's friends started to arrive. I watched as the lady who had been the first to come walked up to one of the sophomores who had just entered the gym.

"You come dance with me," she said, grabbing his hand before he was sure what had happened.

Mike came up to me. "This is fun. Where did they learn to dance like this?"

Mike and many of my students were amazed that some dances actually had set steps and patterns. I joined in as the senior citizens taught us to waltz and polka. I had never learned to dance, either.

One of the seniors who had dressed up for the occasion had on a beautiful long dress with sequins, and the mirrored ball in the middle of the dance floor reflected light off her dress. We danced. She led.

"If I were about sixty years younger, I'd go after you," she said.

I laughed.

"What grade are you in?" she asked.

I laughed harder. "I'm a teacher here. I'm in charge of these kids."

"Oh," she said, "you're so young and handsome."

I didn't laugh. "And you are very beautiful," I said.

"Oh, come on now...."

The orchestra began to play a song from My Fair Lady, and as I followed my partner, I thought of Eliza Doolittle. Henry Higgins saw an elegant woman when everyone else saw a peasant.

"I could have danced all night...." My partner sang along with the music. "That was a good movie," she added, "but I bet it's before your time."

"No, I remember it well." I looked about at my students, everyone of them dancing with a senior citizen.

One older man was teaching a sophomore girl how to waltz. I watched her. I was used to seeing her in torn blue jeans. She was beautiful in a long dress.

When the evening finally came to an end, no one wanted to leave.

Mike walked up to me. "That was the most fun I've ever had in high school."

"You mean that was more fun than your junior-senior proms?" I asked.

"No question about it." Mike was definite.

"What made this so much fun?" I asked.

Without thinking for even a moment, Mike answered, "It really feels good to do something for somebody else."

The following Monday, Paul Harvey, who must have spies all about, concluded his broadcast with this story: "Remember last week I told you about how the Brainerd, Minnesota, student council was going to host a prom for senior citizens? Well, they did...and more than five hundred senior citizens showed up. The high school students danced with the seniors, and the chaperons report no major problems.... Oh, there was a little smooching in the corner, but no major problems. Paul Harvey, good day!"

Tori's Last Chance

JEANNIE ST. JOHN TAYLOR

ori sat on the track at the district meet and leaned into a pre-race stretch. Through all four years of high school, she had faithfully sweated through her twenty miles a week. Then, after the other runners went home, she sprinted intervals with her coach. But she had never won a district race. And only district winners went to the finals at State. This race was her last chance.

In the next lane, Kate, a senior from a competing school, sprinted up her lane and back. She looked tense. Kate had never made it to state either. This was Kate's last chance, too.

"Nervous?" Kate asked.

Tori nodded and jogged in place. "You?"

Kate nodded. "Races upset my stomach."

An official in a black shirt announced, "Ladies, take your marks."

"See you at the finish line," Kate said as they positioned themselves in their lanes.

"I'll be there," said Tori. She knew she had to beat Kate to win.

"Get set." The official pointed the gun upward.

Lord, help me do my best. Tori prayed. *Let this race bring glory to you.* Bang! The race started.

Tori ran just behind Kate, as Coach had instructed, listening to the sound of Kate's breathing and the pounding of feet on the track. She planned to stick close to Kate's shoulder for the first three laps, then sprint past her in the final stretch.

"Perfect pace!" Coach yelled from the sidelines in the second lap.

Tori felt confident, strong.

Kate pulled ahead. Tori relaxed into her stride, placing one foot in front of the other in a steady rhythm. There'd be plenty of time to pass Kate in the last lap.

By the time Tori finished the second lap, the pack of runners had already fallen half a track behind. *No need to worry about them,* she thought. *I'll just glide behind Kate, then pass her when Coach gives the signal.*

Near the end of the third lap, Coach signaled.

Okay, Kate, Tori thought, *it's just you and me now.* She strode out, closing the distance between them. Kate must have sensed it. She glanced back at Tori, a sure sign she was tired.

Tori pumped her arms and legs, pulling up beside Kate.

She and Kate ran side by side now, their breathing nearly drowning out the roar of the crowd. The bell sounded as they rounded the turn into the final lap.

Two more steps and Tori surged past Kate. She glimpsed Kate's face as she passed. Kate looked pale and sick—the way Tori had felt her freshman year when she collapsed at the finish line.

Tori knew she had her! The crowd thundered in triumph!

Then somehow, out of nowhere, Kate ran beside her again on the outside, passing her. Kate's breathing sounded in rasping gasps. She exhaled in grunts.

"No!" screamed Coach, "don't let her pass you! Push harder."

Tori willed her legs to move faster, but they wouldn't. As though in slow motion she watched Kate move two, then three strides ahead of her. Almost at the finish line, Kate suddenly pitched forward and fell face down on the track, her body pushed to exhaustion.

I'm the winner! Tori thought. For a split second she exulted in her victory. Then she stopped cold, her feet inches from the finish line.

No, she thought, *I won't win this way.*

She bent down, struggling for breath, and grabbed Kate's legs. Kate was unconscious. Tori planned to pull Kate's legs over the finish line, giving Kate the first place she deserved, then she'd step over. But now she could see the pack of runners bearing down on them.

Kate's legs, slippery with sweat, slid from Tori's hands. The other runners rapidly approached. Tori grabbed Kate under the arms. As she dragged Kate over the line she felt the *whoosh! whoosh! whoosh!* of three runners crossing the finish line. Had she pulled Kate across in time?

Kate's trainer ran over to help. Kate opened her eyes. Tori paced with her hands on her hips, getting her breathing under control. She tried not to cry.

An official leaned down and handed Kate the first place marker. Tori smiled at Kate.

Another official held out the second place marker to Tori. "Congratulations," he said. "You're going to State."

"What?" Tori asked, confused.

"First and second place winners compete at state this year," he said. "Didn't you know?"

Tori smiled again. "God is good."

For the Love of Strangers

ROBIN JONES GUNN
FROM VIRTUE MAGAZINE

Alenka taught me everything about hospitality.

Petite Alenka with heart-shaped face and clear, silver-gray eyes. Alenka, the Russian. She taught me, all right. But I was not an easy student.

We met in Austria in the home of a Christian family. I'd been there for several days, biding my time until school started. One night, Alenka arrived at the doorstep. She stood shivering in the doorway of this remote farmhouse looking like a frightened mouse.

The family greeted her with such joy and excitement. There was something special about this young girl, and I wanted to be in on the celebration. But as I listened to all the chatter, I realized I couldn't understand a single word.

"What is she saying?" I finally asked Karl, the oldest son. "It's Russian," he whispered. "She speaks only Russian."

"But what is she saying?"

"She's had a hard go of it. We didn't think she'd make it. She really needs to rest. We'll put her in the guest room with you. She'll have to share your bed."

Share my bed? I didn't even know her! Where did she come from? What was she doing here?

I followed Karl as he carried her small brown satchel to the guest room.

"Why is she here?" I persisted. "Did she defect or something? What's her name?"

Karl paused for a moment, then looking directly at me he answered, "Her name is Alenka. That's all you need to know." His eyes told me he meant it. I didn't say another word.

That night I went to bed with a stranger beside me.

She slept well. A deep, soundless, motionless sleep with the white down comforter pulled up securely under her chin. I slept very little and rose early to help in the kitchen. My host family had eight children. That made for twelve places at the large wooden dinner table as they opened their family circle to include Alenka and me.

Alenka didn't make it to breakfast nor did she make it to dinner at noon. But later that afternoon while I was washing potatoes in the kitchen, she came in and smiled.

She looked like a tiny wildflower. Fresh, inviting. She spoke freely with clever hand gestures and facial expressions, and I figured out she must be starving. When I set a bowl of stew and a piece of bread before her, she ate slowly, gracefully, as if giving thanks for each morsel.

That night, when we went to bed, she slipped out of our room and returned with a cup of steaming tea for me, but nothing for herself. I propped myself up in bed, dumbfounded at her kindness. Speaking in Russian she urged me to drink it, and all the while I sipped she spoke freely in her animated way. I had no idea what she was telling me.

The next night she brought me a piece of thick brown bread smeared with pale dairy butter. I think she may have saved her piece from supper. Along with the bread she brought a glass of sweet berry juice. This time she crossed her legs on the thick comforter and sat up straight. The moon-light fell on her hands, folded daintily in her lap. Then tilting her chin up, she sang to me as I ate. It was painfully beautiful—like lonely flute notes on the still night air.

I felt so inadequate to receive her graciousness and so clumsy at trying to communicate with her. I spoke to Karl about it after breakfast the next morning. Why was she doing these nice things for me? I knew she was also a Christian, but we were strangers, foreigners. According to our governmental policies, we were enemies.

"Do you know real hospitality?" Karl asked.

I thought about the style of entertaining I'd grown up with in my California home. The kind that requires china and crystal and hors d'oeuvres and decorates the bathroom with monogrammed towels. Then I thought about Alenka's gifts and her song in the night.

"I don't know," I stammered. "Maybe I don't."

"Hospitality literally means 'the love of strangers,'" Karl explained. "That's what Alenka is doing. Loving you—a stranger."

Me? A stranger? I'm not the stranger, she is!

The thought bothered me all afternoon, and as soon as I could get away, I took a brisk walk into the deep woods to sort it all out. The late summer twigs snapped beneath my feet, and the branches that brushed me felt scratchy and brittle.

I came upon a small clearing where the sun poured through like carameled syrup and covered a handmade wooden bench. The sun-drenched bench felt good on my back.

I basked in the warmth as I took inventory of my concept of hospitality.

My picture of a well-orchestrated social event designed to impress my friends didn't match up with what Karl said about hospitality being the "love of strangers." Perhaps I didn't know real hospitality. Perhaps I didn't know real love.

Just then I heard a sound of someone else walking into the woods. Into the clearing stepped Alenka. She looked like a fairy-tale character with wildflowers in her amber hair and her skirt clutched up in front of her. Speaking brightly, she offered me wild strawberries from the batch cradled tenderly in her bunched up skirt.

Then Alenka touched my shoulder and anxiously pointed behind me. She whispered and indicated that I should turn around to see something. I slowly turned to see a deer standing no more than six feet away. He stood perfectly staunch, eyeing us, the two strangers in his domain. Suddenly he turned and ran cutting off our brief encounter, leaving us alone. Alenka giggled a joyful, girlish giggle, and I thought how unlike the deer she was. She hadn't bolted when we were thrust together. She came to me warm and fast with a heart of love.

"You are my friend," I told her as we marched back together through the crackling tinder. "You have taught me a lot." I think she understood.

Alenka was already asleep when I went to bed that night. It was my last night, and I'd stayed up late talking to our host family. On my pillow rested a wooden bowl of berries. Alenka's treasured wild strawberries. Next to the bowl rested a handmade card. I opened it with tears in my eyes. Three tiny yellow wildflowers were carefully pressed inside. Opposite the flowers Alenka had written five Russian words in bold black letters and then signed her name. I held that card for a long time in the darkened room while Alenka slept peacefully beside me.

In the years that followed, I held that card many times with treasured thoughts of Alenka. I never had the words translated into English. Their message was already clear to me. They said the same thing Alenka had been saying since we met—

"Dear Stranger, I Love You. Alenka"

Driving Lessons

CHARLES SWINDOLL
FROM *THE GRACE AWAKENING*

I remember when I first earned my license to drive. I was about sixteen, as I recall. I'd been driving off and on for three years (scary thought, isn't it?). My father had been with me most of the time during my learning experiences, calmly sitting alongside me in the front seat, giving me tips, helping me know what to do. My mother usually wasn't in on those excursions because she spent more of her time biting her nails (and screaming) than she did advising. My father was a little more easygoing. Loud noises and screeching brakes didn't bother him nearly as much. My grandfather was the best of all. When I would drive his car, I would hit things...*Boom!* He'd say stuff like, "Just keep on going, Bud. I can buy more fenders, but I can't buy more grandsons. You're learning." What a great old gentleman. After three years of all that nonsense I finally earned my license.

I'll never forget the day I came in, flashed my newly acquired permit, and said, "Dad, look!" He exclaimed, "Whoa! Look at this. You got your license. Good for you!" Holding the keys to his car, he tossed them in my direction and smiled, "Tell you what, son...you can have the car for two hours, all on your own." Only four words, but how wonderful: "All on your own."

I thanked him, danced out to the garage, opened the car door, and shoved the key into the ignition. My pulse rate must have shot up to 180 as I backed out of the driveway and roared off. While cruising along "all on my own," I began to think wild stuff—like, *This car can probably do 100 miles an hour. I could go to Galveston and back twice in two hours if I averaged 100 miles an hour. I can fly down the Gulf freeway and even run a few lights. After all, nobody's here to say, "Don't!"* We're talking dangerous, crazy thoughts! But you know what? I didn't do any of them. I don't believe I drove above the speed limit. In fact, I distinctly remember turning into the driveway early…didn't even stay away the full two hours. Amazing, huh? I had my dad's car all to myself with a full gas tank in a context of total privacy and freedom, but I didn't go crazy. Why? My relationship with my dad and my granddad was so strong that I couldn't, even though I had a license and nobody was in the car to restrain me. Over a period of time there had developed a sense of trust, a deep love relationship.

After tossing me the keys, my dad didn't rush out and tape a sign on the dashboard of the car, "Don't you dare drive beyond the speed limit" or "Cops are all around the city, and they'll catch you, boy, so don't even think about taking a risk." He simply smiled and said, "Here are the keys, son, enjoy it." What a demonstration of grace. And did I ever enjoy it!

Dream Date

LARRY ANDERSON
FROM *TAKING THE TRAUMA OUT OF TEEN TRANSITIONS*

Carl had dreamed of his prom for months. He couldn't wait for the night to actually arrive. Cindy, the girl he had always wanted to date, had said yes. Carl's feet had not touched the ground since. This was going to be the most romantic night on record. *Cindy will be so completely swept off her feet she'll be putty in my strong, manly hands*, thought Carl with a mental swagger. From now through eternity, when young people dream of true love and romance, the story of Carl and Cindy will be their example.

As he dressed for the big date, Carl rehearsed each moment of the evening. Every word he would say, each move he would make, were carefully and thoughtfully choreographed. Nothing was going to spoil this evening.

He pulled up in front of Cindy's house in his mom's newly washed and waxed car. As he approached the front door he frantically went over the mental notes he had made on how to react to her new dress and how to win over her parents with his maturity and charm. Overall, Carl was pleased with how this first stage went as he led Cindy to the car. He had endured the photo session and had made polite and articulate conversation with Cindy's folks.

He opened the car door for Cindy and his heart leaped to his throat as he thought of driving alone to dinner. As he scooted behind the wheel and turned the key in the ignition the nightmare began. The car wouldn't start. With Cindy in the car and her entire family watching from the living room window, Carl tried to be nonchalant. He turned the key again. Nothing. Then he got out of the car and raised the hood hoping that this act might create some self-healing magic.

Still nothing.

As he got back into the car his eyes riveted on his mistake. In his excitement to pick up Cindy he had forgotten to put the car in park. He coughed and tried to distract Cindy as he quickly put the console gearshift back to P. When he looked up, Cindy was giggling and to his horror so was her entire family.

Carl's heart began to sink as he drove away.

Dinner took forever. The service was slow and the waiter, weary of high schoolers' tips was not greatly helpful. Carl kept wondering, *Why, when you are paying so much more does the service get progressively worse?* Conversation was stiff, and Carl began to long for the crowded prom with its noise and familiar faces. He barely had enough money for dinner and for a fleeting second pondered what it would be like to have to ask Cindy for help.

By the time they got to the dance it was just about over. Still, it was an unmatched thrill for Carl to escort Cindy to the dance floor. He felt every eye in the place on them as he used the steps he had rehearsed for hours alone in his bedroom.

After the dance came the party. A good friend of Carl's was hosting the affair, and Carl was anxious to see his buddies there. He picked up a plate of munchies for the two of them and headed back to where Cindy was sitting with some friends.

He forget about the step. There was a step down into the next room and missing that step was disastrous. He went head first toward the floor and landed face down in the plate of food. Some of his friends thought "Crazy Carl" had done it on purpose, and his misstep actually turned out to be the highlight of the party.

All the way home Cindy assured her dejected suitor that she had had a wonderful time. As Carl walked her to the door he had one more chance for true love: a good-night kiss. He stood shyly at the front door like a first-grader meeting an adult for the first time. Just as they were about to embark on that epic kiss Cindy spoke up, "Carl, isn't that your mother's car rolling down the street?"

First in stunned amazement, then in panic, he saw the car rolling down the hill toward a truck. He sprinted into the street and quickly grabbed the door of his runaway vehicle.

It was locked.

The car continued to roll as Carl fished the keys from his pocket, unlocked the door, jumped in, and stopped it about one foot from the truck.

Carl was panting, sweating, and humiliated. He started the car and began to turn, hoping to go home and never be seen again. He heard a tap on the window. Cindy was standing outside the car. He rolled down the window, red and sweating, and looked into the eyes of the girl of his now-shattered dreams.

Then in an instant his world was turned back around. Cindy looked down at Carl, told him again that she had had a very nice time, leaned through the window, and gave him a kiss on the cheek.

Life can be beautiful.

Magical Moments

RHONDA MARCKS

first met Taylor in my school cafeteria over breakfast. My community outreach team was having a meeting to introduce the new members. As usual I was one of the first to arrive and was enjoying my omelet when our team leader and a very handsome, blond, blue-eyed man sat down across from me. "Hey Rhonda, I'd like you to meet Taylor—he'll be joining our team this semester."

As Taylor and I shook hands I was dumbfounded at the slight tingling I felt shoot up my arm. "Surely," I thought, "that only happens in the movies and romance novels!" Yet, there I was with an arm that was still tingling even after he had let it go. I tried to calm myself down and act normal while I finished eating my breakfast. Thank goodness it was only a few minutes later that the rest of the team and the two other new members sat down at the table.

All during the meeting I only half listened to Steven discuss the ideas he had for this semester. I was trying to figure out what to do with these feelings I had for Taylor. A year before I had allowed myself to fall for a friend of mine and it turned out disastrous and I didn't want to repeat that experience. I decided then and there in the midst of a noisy cafeteria that I wouldn't let myself fall for Taylor no matter what happened.

Nevertheless it was only a month later that my pact crumbled to pieces. I had been so proud of myself holding back on my feelings even when I found out Taylor and I shared the same major—art. If it hadn't been for that one Saturday night after the team finished up one of our teen chapel services I would have been home free. They say God moves in mysterious ways, and boy did I learn that in a flash.

It all started during chapel when Melanie was leading praise and worship. All of a sudden she couldn't sing. She started shaking her head and had to hand the microphone over to Steven to finish. I watched as she walked out of the chapel area still shaking her head. I realized that she was having a panic attack. I had had a few of them myself and it wasn't a fun thing to experience. I wanted to go run after her and talk to her but I was needed in the service so I had to wait.

After the service was over and everyone was walking out I noticed Melanie sitting in the back pew. I worked up all my courage and went to sit next to her. She looked up at me and seemed shocked that I'd come to talk to her. I explained to her what I had felt watching her go through the attack and let her know I understood. She relaxed instantly and began opening up to me about some situations she was going through.

"Well," one might ask, "what does this have to do with Taylor?" It has everything to do with him. You see, over the few minutes I talked with Melanie I realized in many ways she could have been my twin. We sat there talking for several minutes and I was disappointed when one after another of my team members just passed us not even asking Melanie if she was okay.

Then it happened! My heart flipped. I was listening to Melanie when out of the corner of my eye I saw Taylor walking toward us. I was overwhelmed and almost cried in happiness when he actually sat down in the pew in front of us. He asked Melanie if she was okay and told her how his heart had ached when he saw how stressed she had been. I sat there listening as he consoled her and actually got her to laugh.

My heart gave a groan and it was at that moment that I realized I was lost. He had broken every wall I had tried to place between my good sense and my heart. I had no choice but to give in and allow my love for him to grow and flourish. Over the following months I learned what real love was. I found out that it wasn't some good feeling I would get when everything was smooth sailing, but it was the calm, peaceful, and sure feeling I felt no matter what was going on.

Five years have gone by since that night when I lost all reasoning and found my heart. Even now, as I'm typing this my heart is overflowing with magical memories and love for Taylor. Granted, it hasn't all been roses and daisies, but like many things in life those times seem to fade in the background. I can honestly say, though, that even if I live to be a hundred years old I'll never forget that first time he took my hand and then my heart. Forever.

Of More Value

JERRY B. JENKINS
FROM *STILL THE ONE*

A friend, the father of two daughters, admits he doesn't mind putting a little fear into the boys. His daughters may be embarrassed when he asks for a few moments alone with their dates, and he might rather the young men think he's an okay guy than that he's a mean, protective father. But some things are worth a little awkwardness. Boys might think such dads are a little overprotective. To the fathers of daughters, however, there is no such thing as overprotective.

Another friend says he uses a sports car analogy to get his point across. He'll say to the boy, "If I owned the most expensive, exotic sports car on the road and I let you take it for a spin, you'd be careful with it, wouldn't you?"

"Oh, yes, sir, you bet."

"You'd treat it better than if it were your own, wouldn't you?"

"Yes, sir."

"I wouldn't want to think you were screeching the tires, would I?"

"No, sir."

"Well, let me tell you something, just so we're straight with each other, man to man. My daughter is of infinitely more value to me than any car could be. Do you get my drift? She's on loan from me to you for the next few hours, and I wouldn't want to discover that she was treated with any less care or respect than I would give her. I'm responsible for her. She's mine. I'm entrusting her to you. That trust brooks no second chances. Understand?"

By then, of course, the young man is wondering why he didn't ask someone else out. He's only nodding, unable to speak. Most often, he brings the girl home earlier than promised. The daughter might even complain about her father's approach, but deep down she feels loved and cherished, and you can be sure she'll marry a man who treats her that way.

Looking Back

Looking back on high school years
Hopes, dreams, laughter and tears
We've struggled, we've triumphed
We've lost and we've won
But through it all we still had fun.

—Jessica Smith-Blockley and Meghan Roberts
Graduation speech, Mountain View High School

The New Kid

★

FROM MORE RANDOM ACTS OF KINDNESS

I was the new kid at my high school and, being very shy, I found it hard to make friends. My escape was volleyball. I love to play and was good enough to get on the girls' varsity team. Most of the girls on the team were pretty nice, but they had been playing together for three years and I was clearly the outsider. The third game of the season was our biggest challenge; we had to play the state champions and they had an absolutely awesome player on their team named Angela.

We knew we didn't have much chance but we at least wanted to play well. I think I played okay, but I don't remember doing anything that special. Anyway, we lost, but we forced the match to go three games and were even ahead for a little while. When we were collecting our stuff after the game, Angela walked up, pointed her finger right at me, and said, "You are good, girl!" Then she smiled and walked away.

I was so surprised I was almost embarrassed until my whole team came running over to hug me. On the way back to the bus, one of my teammates turned to me and said, "Next year we'll beat them, because Angela is graduating and we've still got you."

In The Dugout

During a long and losing baseball game,
the restless twelve-year-old players were
questioning Ritchie, their assistant coach,
about his attractive younger sister.
Annoyed at the idle chatter, the head coach hollered,
"When you're in the dugout, talk baseball!"
After a moment's silence, a young voice began,
"So, Ritchie, does your sister play baseball?"

—*Jack Eppolito*
from Christian Reader *magazine*

Live!

EMILY CAMPAGNA
GRADUATION SPEECH
MOUNTAIN VIEW HIGH SCHOOL

Live. Love and cherish life.

Make friends, memories, and plans.

Your life is about you, but life is not about you.

Fall in love.

Love the fall and winter and spring and summer.

Ski, skate, sing, and dance.

Smell the rain and the chocolate chip cookies.

Take all the time you need, but don't waste it.

Catch the big one with your dad.

Go on that trip with your mom.

Love children, for you were once one.

Learn from your elders, and one day you'll have their wisdom.

Seek the truth. Find it in yourself, others, and the God of your faith.

Be patient and gentle.

Most of all, truly live.

Seeing Each Other in a Different Light

SUSAN MANEGOLD
FROM WOMAN'S WORLD MAGAZINE

When my daughters were little, we loved to spend time together talking or watching TV. But by the time Lauren and Carly were teens, they preferred being in their own rooms, talking on the phone or listening to music, to being with me—or even each other.

I knew it was just a part of their growing up, but while I wanted my daughters to be independent, I also wanted them to be close, and a part of me missed the days when we'd all curl up on the couch with a bowl of popcorn.

Then one windy night while their dad was working, the lights went out. "Cool!" I heard Carly, thirteen, call from her room.

"I hate this!" Lauren, eighteen, cried.

Grabbing candles and a flashlight, I headed for the girls' rooms. Lauren's was already filled with the cozy glow of candlelight, so Carly and I filed in, and soon we were all snuggled on Lauren's bed.

Carly was excited, but Lauren pouted when Carly suggested, "Let's tell stories." As Carly began to talk about school and her friends, however,

Lauren's pout disappeared. She snuggled closer to Carly, and soon they were giggling just like they had when they were younger.

I could tell from the sparkle in Carly's eyes that she knew the darkness had brought us a gift, but I wondered if Lauren felt the same way. Suddenly, Lauren's phone rang. "Yeah, our power is out too," she told her friend. "But I'll have to call you back. I'm hanging out with my mom and my sister."

She knows it too! I thought. And after she hung up, she offered, "Let's sing songs." Tears filled my eyes.

A short while later, the power came back on. "Oh no!" the girls groaned. But since then, we've all felt closer. We hug more, and the girls don't tease each other as much. Some nights we just sit and talk. The power outage didn't just leave us in the dark; it gave us the opportunity to see each other in a different light.

Making a Difference

Things I've Learned Lately...

It's always better to give people the
benefit of the doubt, most of us don't,
Dog's eyes show their trust and love,
People are precious,
And the "greatest of these" really is love.

Goodwill

CYNTHIA HAMOND

Annie leaned against her locker and sighed. What a day! What a disaster! This school year wasn't starting out the way she had planned it at all.

Of course, Annie hadn't planned on that new girl, Kristen. And she definitely hadn't planned on the new girl wearing the exact same skirt that Annie was supposed to be wearing.

It wasn't just any skirt. Annie had baby-sat three active brothers all summer to buy that skirt and its designer accent top. When she saw them in her *Teen Magazine*, Annie knew they were meant for her. She had gone right to the phone and called the 800 number for the "outlet nearest" her.

With price and picture in hand, she had set off to convince her mother.

"It's great, hon." Her mother agreed. "I just can't see spending as much on one outfit as I do for all your clothes." Annie wasn't surprised, but she was disappointed.

"Well, if it's that important, we could put it on layaway," her mom said. "You'd have to pay for it though."

So, she did. Every Friday, Annie took all her baby-sitting money and paid down the balance. She had made her final payment just last week and hurried home to try on the skirt and top. The moment or truth had arrived and she was afraid to look. She stood in front of the mirror with her eyes squeezed shut. She counted to three and forced herself to open them.

It was perfect from the side from the back and even from the front, it was perfect. She walked, she sat, and she turned. She practiced humbly taking compliments so her friends wouldn't think she was stuck-up.

The next day, Annie and her mother gave her room the end of summer "good going over." They washed and ironed the bedspread and curtains and vacuumed behind and under everything.

Then they sorted through the closets and drawers for clothes to give away. Annie dreaded all the tugging on and pulling off, the laundering and the folding it all into boxes. Lastly, they dropped the boxes off at Goodwill and headed to her grandmother's for the weekend.

When they got home Sunday night, Annie ran straight to her bedroom. Everything had to be just right for her "Grand Entrance" at school the next day.

She flung open her closet and pulled out her top and her... and her... skirt? It wasn't there. "It has to be here!" But it wasn't.

"Dad! Mom!" Annie's search became frantic. Her parents rushed in. Hangers and clothes were flying everywhere.

"My skirt! It isn't here!" Annie stood there with her top in one hand and an empty hanger in the other.

"Now, Annie." Her dad tried to calm her. "It didn't just get up and walk away. We'll find it." But they didn't. For two hours they searched through closets and drawers, the laundry room, under the bed and in the bed. It just wasn't there.

Annie sank into bed that night trying to figure out the puzzle.

When she woke up that morning she felt tired and dull. She picked out something...anything...to wear. Nothing measured up to her summer daydreams.

It was at her school locker that the puzzle became, well, more puzzling. "You're Annie, right?" A voice came from behind her.

Annie turned. Shock waves hit her and her thoughts muddled. THAT'S my skirt. That's MY skirt! That's my SKIRT?

"I'm Kristen. The principal gave me the locker next to yours. She thought since we lived on the same block and I'm new here, you could show me around." Her voice trailed off, unsure. Annie just stared. How?...Where?...Is that my...?

Kristen felt uneasy. "You don't have to. I told her we didn't really know each other. We've only seen each other on the sidewalk."

That was true. Annie and Kristen had passed each other. Annie to and from her sitting job and Kristen in her fast food uniform that smelled of onions and grease at the end of the day. Annie pulled her thoughts back to Kristen's words.

"Sure. I'll be happy to show you around," Annie said, not happy at all. All day, friends gushed over Kristen and THE SKIRT while Annie stood by with a still smile.

And now Annie was waiting to walk Kristen home, hoping to sort this out.

They chatted all the way to Annie's house before she worked up the nerve to ask the big question. "Where did you get your skirt, Kristen?"

"Isn't it beautiful? My mom and I saw it in a magazine while we were waiting for my grandma at the doctor's office."

"Oh, your mom bought it for you."

"Well, no." Kristen lowered her voice. "We've had kind of a hard time lately. Dad lost his job and my grandma was sick. We moved here to take care of her while my dad looked for work."

All that went right over Annie's head. "You must have saved most of your paycheck then."

Kristen blushed. "I saved all my money and gave it to my mom to buy school clothes for my brother and sister."

Annie couldn't stand it. "Where did you get your skirt?"

Kristen stammered. "My mother found it at Goodwill in a box that was dropped off just as she got there. Mom opened it and there was the skirt from the magazine, brand new, with the tags still on it." Kristen looked up.

Goodwill? Brand new? The puzzle pieces fell into place.

Kristen smiled and her face glowed. "My mother knew it was meant for me. She knew it was a blessing."

"Kristen...I," Annie stopped. This wasn't going to be easy. "Kristen," Annie tried again, "can I tell you something?"

"Sure. Anything."

"Kristen." Annie took in a deep breath. "Do you have a minute to come up to my room? I think I have a top that would go great with your skirt."

Little Lies

MEREDITH PROOST
FROM *TREASURES: STORIES & ART BY STUDENTS IN OREGON*

It all began one Tuesday when my sister Melinda and I lost all track of time and found we couldn't possibly finish practicing our piano lessons before our mom came home from grocery shopping. Before she left, we had agreed to do all our chores and practice piano.

"Yes," we said together when Mom asked if we had finished our practicing. But when she walked into the living room, there was the piano music, stacked just as she had stacked it that morning. And the lesson book was on the table where we had left it after our piano lesson the day before.

Mom knew we were lying. She had a sad look on her face. Before Melinda or I could make up an excuse, Mom told us that she was going to tell us a lie sometime during the next few days. We wouldn't know when she was lying, and the lie would be something very important to both of us.

That night Mom told us that the next morning when we woke up, breakfast would be waiting: hot cereal with lots of cream and even more brown sugar, just the way we like it. Melinda and I looked at each other knowingly. That must be the lie.

But the next morning when we woke up, in the kitchen we found our bowls of hot cereal with lots of cream and even more brown sugar, just the way we like it.

On Wednesday, Mom told us that she would pick us up right after school so that we could go shopping for spring clothes. Melinda and I looked at each other knowingly and said to ourselves that had to be the lie. We decided we would be going home on the bus as usual.

But after school, there sat Mom in the parking lot ready to take us shopping.

The following day our dad was on a business trip. Mom told us to pick a restaurant, Italian or Chinese, and the three of us would go out for dinner that night. Melinda and I looked at each other knowingly. That must be the lie. If we said Chinese, Mom would take us out for pizza. If we said Italian, we knew we'd be having chow mein for dinner.

We said, "Chinese," and that night we had won ton soup, chow mein, fortune cookies, and tea.

When we arrived home from school Friday, Mom greeted us with, "Guess what! I just reserved two airplane tickets. You two get to fly—all by yourselves—to visit your grandma over spring vacation." Now that is something we had always wanted to do. We had dreamed about traveling alone and talked about it for years. Ordinarily we would have run to our rooms to start packing, even though spring vacation was three weeks away. But we looked at each other knowingly. That had to be the lie.

Mom may have been surprised at our lack of excitement but she didn't say a word. She waited until the following day to ask us if we had discovered her lie.

Melinda said, "Yes, we know. We won't be flying to Grandma's for spring vacation. Everything else you have said has been true, so the airplane trip must be the lie."

"I'm glad it's finally over," I said.

Melinda said, "Yes. It has been awful for days thinking we couldn't trust you. I guess we deserved that little lie about flying to Grandma's."

Mom smiled. "The lie was that I would tell you a lie," she said softly. "I haven't told you any lies. The tickets to Grandma's are under your pillow. Sweet dreams."

Look Again

So many times all that is discussed is the wrongdoing of kids.
However, the successes and goodness of all of us
far outweigh the few problems that get magnified so greatly.

—Ryan Timm
Graduation speech, Bend High School

Standing Tall

STEVE FARRAR
FROM *STANDING TALL*

When I was a sophomore in high school, we moved to a new town and a new high school. It was the typical scenario of being the new kid who didn't know anyone. One of the fastest ways to make friends in that situation is to go out for a sport. In about two days you know more guys from playing ball than you could meet in three months.

Normally, I would have gone out for basketball. But I had done something very foolish. I had brought home a "D" on my last report card. The only reason I had gotten a "D" was that I had horsed around in the class and basically exhibited some very irresponsible behavior in turning in papers. My dad had a rule for the three boys in our family, and the rule was this: if any of us got anything lower than a "C" in a class, we couldn't play ball. He didn't demand that we get straight "A's" or make the honor roll. My dad knew that the only reason any of us would get a "D" was that we were fooling around instead of acting in a responsible way.

As a result, I didn't go out for basketball. Now my dad was all for me playing ball. He had been all-state in both basketball and football in high school, went to college on a basketball scholarship, and after World War II, was offered a contract to play football for the Pittsburgh Steelers. He wanted me to play. But he was more interested in developing my character than he was in developing my jump shot. My dad had some long-term goals for me that were more important than basketball. He knew it would be very good for me to have to live with the consequence of sitting out a basketball season due to my lackadaisical behavior.

One day I was in my physical education class, and we were playing basketball. I didn't know it but the varsity coach was in the bleachers watching the pickup game. After we went into the locker room he came up to me and asked me who I was and why I wasn't out for varsity basketball. I told him that we had just recently moved into town and that I'd come out for basketball next year. He said that he wanted me to come out this year.

I told him that my dad had a rule about getting any grade lower than a "C."

The coach said, "But according to the school rules you're still eligible to play if you have just one 'D'."

"Yes, sir, I realize that," I replied. "But you have to understand that my dad has his own eligibility rules."

"What's your phone number?" the coach asked. "I'm going to call your dad."

I responded, "I'll be happy to give you the phone number, but it will be a waste of your time."

This coach was a big, aggressive guy. He was about six feet two inches and 220 pounds which put him one inch shorter and twenty pounds lighter than my dad. Coach was used to getting his own way. But he hadn't met my dad. I knew before the coach ever called what my dad's answer would be.

Was my dad capable of change? Sure he was. Was he going to change because he got a call from the varsity coach? Of course not. A lot of dads would have been so flattered that they would have compromised on the consequences.

That night after dinner Dad told me the coach had called. He told me he had told the coach no. He then reminded me of the importance of being responsible in class and that he really wanted me to play basketball. But the ball was in my court (no pun intended). If I wanted to play ball it was up to me. At that point, I was very motivated to work hard in class so that I could play basketball the next season.

The next morning the coach came up to me in the locker room.

"I talked to your dad yesterday afternoon and he wouldn't budge. I explained the school eligibility rules, but he wouldn't change his mind. I don't have very much respect for your father."

I couldn't believe my ears. *This coach didn't respect my father.* Even I had enough sense to know my dad was doing the right thing. Sure, I wanted to play ball but I knew my dad was a man of his word and he was right in not letting me play. I couldn't believe this coach would say such a thing.

"Coach," I said. "I can tell you that I highly respect my dad. And I also want you to know that I will never play basketball for you."

I never did. I got my grades up, but I never went out for varsity basketball. I refused to play for a man who didn't respect my dad for doing what was right. That was the end of my high school basketball career because the man coached basketball for my remaining years in high school.

Why wouldn't I play for him? Because he didn't respect my father. If he didn't have the sense to respect my dad then I sure as heck wasn't going to play for him. Come to think of it, the real reason I wouldn't join his team was that I didn't respect *him.* He was a compromiser and I suspected that he would do anything to win. My dad was a man of conviction and a man of character. And any coach who couldn't see that was not the kind of man I wanted to associate with. My dad was strict and unwilling to change his conviction even though it hurt him for me not to play ball. My dad was capable of change, but he was unwilling to change because he had a long-term objective for my life that the coach didn't have.

The coach wanted to win games.

My dad wanted to build a son.

i Should Have Said Something...

CHRISTY SIMON
FROM *CAMPUS LIFE* MAGAZINE

Writing class started out harmlessly enough that day. I was sitting there, scribbling notes as the teacher lectured.

Nothing out of the ordinary there. But then it happened. The teacher introduced the topic of "appropriate word choices in everyday writing." As soon as he'd mentioned the topic, a student raised his hand and with a big grin, asked, "May I recite the seven dirty words *not* to use?"

I got the feeling he didn't want to do it for the sake of "education." I was sure the teacher would put a quick end to his "little joke."

I was wrong.

"Would anyone be offended?" the teacher asked casually.

No hands shot up. No one said anything.

So my classmate reeled off his list of seven dirty words. He not only did it once. He did it twice.

The clock had never ticked more slowly than it did the twenty seconds it took to repeat the words. The teacher remained quiet. The class snickered and then cheered, like he'd done something great. I turned away and stared at my notebook. My head began spinning, and a sick feeling crept into the pit of my stomach. *You should've said something,* I chided myself.

It wasn't as though I'd never heard dirty words. I had—in the locker room, in the hallway, in the cafeteria. And usually, there wasn't much I could do other than ignore them and keep moving.

But this was different. In this particular situation, I didn't have to hear those words. My teacher had given me the choice. I could've raised my hand and said, "Yes, I'd be offended." But I didn't.

As bad as I felt, I learned something important from that class—something I'll remember a lot longer than the "seven dirty words." By not standing up for what I believe in, I'm letting the world around me rip away a little piece of those things I value most. I'm letting the world take out a small part of my character. True, it's just a little piece. But the pieces begin to add up. Before long, there won't be much left.

That experience made me more determined than ever to take a stand when I feel I must. No, it won't always be easy. It may even be embarrassing at times. But at least I'll be able to look at myself in the mirror afterward and say with a smile, "You did what was right."

Call Me

CYNTHIA HAMOND

I know it's here somewhere." Cheryl drops her book bag at her feet so she can dig through her coat pockets. When she dumps her purse out onto the table, everyone waiting in line behind her groans.

Cheryl glances up at the lunch room clock. Only three minutes until the bell and this is the last day to order a yearbook, if you want your name imprinted in gold on the front and Cheryl did, if only she could find her wallet. The line begins to move around her.

"Come on, Cheryl." Darcy might as well stamp her foot, she sounds so impatient. "We'll be late for class."

"Darcy, please!" Cheryl snaps back. Best friends or not, Darcy and Cheryl often frustrate each other. They are just so different. Today is a good example. Darcy had "budgeted" for her yearbook and ordered it the first day of school while Cheryl had almost forgotten...again.

"Darcy, my wallet's gone." Cheryl throws her things back into her purse. "My yearbook money was in it." The bell interrupts her search.

"Someone took it." Darcy, as usual, is quick to point away from the bright side of things.

"Oh, I'm sure I just misplaced it," Cheryl hopes.

They rush into class just before the second bell rings. Darcy takes center stage to Cheryl's problem and happily spreads the news about the theft.

By gym the last hour, Cheryl is tired of being stopped and having to say over and over again, "I'm sure I just left it at home." Rushing into the locker room, she changes quickly and checks the list posted by the field door to see where her group is playing soccer, then hurries out to catch up with them.

The game was a close one, and Cheryl's team is the last one back to the locker room.

Darcy stands waiting for Cheryl by her locker. Cheryl brushes past Juanita, the new girl. It's the shocked look on Darcy's face and the startled gasps of those around her that stop Cheryl.

There, at her feet, is her wallet.

"It fell out of her locker!" Darcy points at Juanita. "She stole it."

Everyone speaks at once.

"The new girl stole it."

"Darcy caught her red-handed."

"I knew there was something about her."

"Report her."

Cheryl turns and looks at Juanita. She's never really noticed her before, beyond her "new girl" label.

Juanita picks up the wallet and holds it out to Cheryl. Her hands are trembling. "I found it in the parking lot. I was going to give it to you before gym, but you were late."

Darcy's words spit anger. "I'm so sure!"

"Really. It's true." Juanita's voice is high and pleading.

Cheryl hesitates. Juanita's eyes begin to fill with tears.

Cheryl reaches for her wallet.

"I'm so glad you found it." Cheryl smiles. "Thanks, Juanita."

The tension around them breaks. "Good thing she found it." Everyone but Darcy agrees.

Cheryl does another quick change and then bangs her locker closed. "Hurry, Darcy. There's just enough time to order a yearbook."

"*If* there is any money left in your wallet."

"Not now, Darcy!"

"You are so naive!"

It isn't until they are standing in line that Cheryl opens her wallet.

"It's all here." Cheryl can't help feeling relieved. A small piece of paper flutters down from her wallet.

"She just didn't have time to empty it yet." Darcy bends down to pick up the note. "I know her type. I had her pegged the first day she came." She hands the note to Cheryl.

Cheryl reads it and then looks up at Darcy. "You had her pegged, all right. Maybe that's the problem. Maybe you spend too much time pegging people."

Darcy grabs the note, reads it and throws it back at Cheryl. "Whatever!" she says and stomps off.

Cheryl reads the note again.

> Cheryl,
> I found your wallet in the parking lot. Hope nothing is missing.
>
> Juanita
> P.S. My number is 555-3218. Maybe you could call me.

And Cheryl did.

Dump Boy

Philip Gulley
FROM *Hometown Tales*

When I was nine, my parents bought a house on the south edge of town on the road to the landfill. A family's station in life could be measured by its proximity to the dump. We were solid middle class and therefore lived beyond most of the dump's stench. Two or three days a month we could smell it, just enough to remind us that we were rich enough to avoid the smell most of the time but not wealthy enough to escape it altogether.

Down the road from us, dumpward, lived an old woman and two children. No man. Just that woman and those two kids in a dirty white house down a long, gravel thread of a lane. Where house ended and dump began was barely discernible.

The boy would walk up the road to play with us. When children play, a natural pecking order evolves—overdog and an underdog. He was the underdog, and we overdogs pointed our barbed arrows of meanness his way. He responded as a cornered dog would, with snarls and bites and lunges, which served to confirm our judgment of him—wild kid, out of control, dump boy.

When things heated up, powerful and potent weapons were unsheathed: "You better leave me alone, or my dad will get you!" This was a weapon he seemed unable to counter. No elevated retort, no "Oh, yeah? Well I'll get my dad, and he'll beat up your dad!" Just silence, a turning away, and a walking dumpward.

I don't remember now how the knowledge came to us, but come to us it did—that his father and mother had been killed and the old woman in the dirty white house was his grandma. I do remember that it had no effect on us; the meanness continued. Despite popular thinking, gentleness is not something we are born with; it is something we are taught, and we had not yet learned it.

The lesson came during a basketball game when an elbow was thrown and dump boy charged my brother...fists flying, rage brimming, right at my brother, who lifted not a hand to defend himself. My brother, who just the week before had chased dump boy back home and hurled rocks, now stood stone-stiff while dump boy battered him. It was an unleashing of fury such as I had never seen, dump boy lashing out at every pain that had ever come his way: the midnight visit of a sheriff's chaplain who explained that Mommy and Daddy wouldn't be coming home, the taunts of children who punished him for his grandma's house, the arrows of meanness which pierce the air and then the soul. Fury raining down.

"Hit him, hit him!" we yelled at my brother. But he raised not a hand, and after a time dump boy tired of the easy kill and went home. We assailed my brother with questions, demanding an explanation for his timidity in battle. He mumbled something about not being able to hit a boy who had lost his parents, that he'd been hit enough as it was.

I did not understand then. And still I struggle with its meaning—how gentleness is never real until fury is aimed our way, how I can be gentle with my infant son but think ill of the eight-item man in the seven-item line at the grocery store. Such little acts turn our hearts from gentleness.

Jesus knew this, knew it not only in his head, but in his heart—that gentleness, of all the fruits, is the hardest to cultivate. How strong our tendency to return the blow, to hurl the rock, to call the name. Until our hearts are likewise broken. Why is it that gentleness must necessarily spring from rocky soil, from hardship, from ground sowed with tears?

One day, I prayed to the Lord to teach me gentleness and sat about, waiting for good to happen. Instead, God showed me sorrow, and thus began my education.

Dump boy moved away the next year. I haven't seen him since. Don't even know if he's alive. I hope his life is sweet, that he married well, that tiny children crowd his lap and call him sweeter names than we did.

Are You Wondering Where Your Son Is?

TIM HANSEL
FROM *WHAT KIDS NEED MOST IN A DAD*

Throughout their lives my mother and dad quietly gave even when they didn't see the results. They both had to make numerous sacrifices as my brother and I were growing up. Mom and Dad both worked two jobs in order to help make ends meet.

My brother, Steve, was a fine student and president of his senior class. I tried to follow in his footsteps, although I had a wilder bent at times. I worked hard to be a good student and a good athlete. I even made student body president, which was partly due to some successes on the football field. In my senior year I was voted "All City" and "All State."

On the night of one of my greatest triumphs, however, I failed my father miserably, and it was then that he demonstrated his ability as a servant leader. We had just won our final football game, which meant that we would be going to the State Championship. Some of us had been informed that we would repeat as all league selections for a second year. We decided that all of this success was worth celebration. So many of us football players got together and truly celebrated—a bit too hard.

Somewhere we had gotten some beer, and according to our high school logic, we thought that the more we drank the more we were celebrating. We drank too much.

A policeman happened to drive by and spot us in a parking lot behind some stores. Doing his job, he came over to investigate and discovered that more than a few of us were quite thoroughly inebriated.

The policeman put in a call for some help. Then, in my opinion, he started pushing around some of my friends. Because I was student body president, I felt it was my job to defend them and I ended up trying to wrestle with the cop. That was not a good idea.

The next thing the cop called for was a paddy wagon. Twenty minutes later we were all on our way to jail. That night was one of the longest I've ever spent. At about five the next morning—just about the time the newspaper was being delivered to our home with my picture in it for being an All City and All State athlete—my parents received a phone call from the chief of police.

"Mr. and Mrs. Hansel, are you wondering where your son is? I'm phoning from the city jail and I would like you to come down here and pick up your son."

I can imagine how long that drive downtown was for my folks. When they arrived, they saw a group of dejected young men. Other parents also arrived and had to face the same kind of disappointment. Their sons, who just a few hours before had been a source of such great pride, had all failed so miserably.

My mom and dad walked in and I'll never forget the moment when their eyes met mine. They must have been wondering if all their sacrifices had been worth it. But they never spoke a word.

We got in the car. The sun was coming up and tears were rolling down my cheeks. Finally, I could take the silence no longer and blurted, "Aren't you going to say something, Dad?"

After a pause that probably seemed longer than it really was, my dad finally spoke. "Sure...let's go home and have some breakfast, *son*."

Those were the only words he uttered. At a time when I had failed him most tragically, he reminded me that I was his son. At a time when I felt the deepest remorse and a total failure, he said, in effect, "Let's get on with it."

In the years that followed, he never once brought up that incident. He simply continued to love me for who I was and who I could be.

A Super Dad? Not really. He had all kinds of rough edges and some very real flaws.

A servant father? Indeed.

Anger is a wind that blows out the mind.

—Robert Ingersal

The Winning Check

FROM GOD'S LITTLE DEVOTIONAL BOOK

*N*ot a lot of press coverage was given to the tough Argentine golfer Robert De Vincenzo, but one story from his life shows his greatness as a person.

After winning a tournament, De Vincenzo received his check on the eighteenth green, flashed a smile for the camera, and then walked alone to the clubhouse. As he went to his car, he was approached by a sad-eyed young woman who said to him, "It's a good day for you, but I have a baby with an incurable disease. It's of the blood, and the doctors say she will die." De Vincenzo paused and then asked, "May I help your little girl?" He then took out a pen, endorsed his winning check, and then pressed it into her hand. "Make some good days for the baby," he said.

A week later as he was having lunch at a country club, a Professional Golfer's Association official approached him, saying, "Some of the boys in the parking lot told me you met a young woman after you won the tournament." De Vincenzo nodded. The official said, "Well, she's a phony. She has no sick baby. She fleeced you, my friend."

The golfer looked up and asked, "You mean that there is no baby who is dying without hope?" This time the PGA official nodded. De Vincenzo grinned and said, "That's the best news I've heard all week."

Significance

We realize that what we are accomplishing
is a drop in the ocean.
But if this drop were not in the ocean,
it would be missed.

—Mother Teresa

Yerr Out!

CLARK COTHERN
FROM *AT THE HEART OF EVERY GREAT FATHER*

My father gave me a great example of self-control when I was a boy watching a church-league softball game.

Dad was forty-three at the time and very active. Though he wasn't known for hitting grand slams, he was good at placing the ball and beating the throw. Singles and doubles were his specialty, and he did the best he could with what he had.

This particular dusty, hot Phoenix evening, Dad poked a good one right over the second basemen's head, and the center fielder flubbed the snag and let the ball bloop between his legs.

My dad saw this as he rounded first base, so he poured on the steam. He was five feet ten inches, 160 pounds, and very fast. He figured that if he sprinted for third and slid, he could beat the throw.

Everyone was cheering as he sent two of his teammates over home plate. The center fielder finally got his feet under him and his fingers around the ball as Dad headed toward third. The throw came as hard and fast as the outfielder could fire it, and Dad started a long slide on that sunbaked infield. Dust flew everywhere.

The ball slammed into the third baseman's glove but on the other side of Dad—the outfield side—away from a clear view by the ump who was still at home plate. Our team's dugout was on the third base side of the diamond, and every one of the players had a clear view of the play.

Dad's foot slammed into third base a solid second before the ball arrived and before the third baseman tagged his leg. But much to the amazement—and then dismay—and then anger—of the team, the umpire, who hesitated slightly before making his call, yelled, "Yerr out!"

Instantly, every member of Dad's team poured onto the field and started shouting at once—Dad's teammates were intent on only one purpose: They wanted to win, and by golly they knew they were *right!*

The two runners who had crossed home plate before Dad was called out had brought the score to within one. If Dad was out—and we all knew he wasn't—his team was robbed of a single run.

With only one inning left, this one bad call could cost them the game.

But just as the fracas threatened to boil over into a mini-riot, Dad silenced the crowd. As the dust settled around him, he held up a hand. "Guys, stop!" he yelled. And then more gently, "There's more at stake here than being right. There's something more important here than winning a game. If the ump says I'm out, I'm *out.*"

And with that, he dusted himself off, limped to the bench to get his glove (his leg was bruised from the slide), and walked back into left field all by himself, ready to begin the last inning. One by one, the guys on his team gave up the argument, picked up their own gloves, and walked out to their positions on the field.

I've got to tell you, I was both bewildered and proud that night. My dad's character was showing, and it sparkled. He may have been dusty, but I saw a diamond standing out there under the lights, a diamond more valuable than all the points his team might have scored.

For a few minutes that evening I was a rich kid, basking in my father's decision to be a man, to hold his tongue instead of wagging it, to settle the dust instead of settling a score. I knew his character at that selfless moment was worth more than all the gold-toned plastic trophies you could buy.

Dad held court that night and the verdict came down hard and he was convicted of being a man...and the evidence that proved it was his powerful use of that awe-inspiring weapon.

Self-control.

Opportunity

Each one of us has an opportunity to change the world,
No matter how big or small of an effect.
We have made and will continue to make
the world a better place to live in.

—Steven Hyde
Graduation speech, Sisters High School

Foolproof

ALAN CLIBURN
FROM WWJD STORIES FOR TEENS

It was Tuesday afternoon and we were heading back to the warehouse, Joel and I. I couldn't believe I was actually getting paid good money just to drive around town, but I wasn't complaining either. There was more than driving involved, of course. Joel and I delivered orders for Office Warehouse, which included furniture like desks and filing cabinets.

On this particular Tuesday the truck was in the shop, so Mr. Kramer let us take one of the company cars. Fortunately there was no furniture to deliver, just packages. One of us could have handled it easily, but Mr. Kramer wanted us both to go.

"Might as well start learning how to do the paperwork, Sam," he told me before we left the warehouse.

The paperwork was a piece of cake. We just had to get somebody to sign for the merchandise at every stop. We had several deliveries in the same vicinity. Maybe that's why we finished so soon.

"Hey, turn left at the next corner," Joel said suddenly. "We've worked hard enough for one afternoon," he went on. "Let's take a little break. Pull up there in front of Harry's." Harry's was a "family recreational center," with video and computer games and stuff like that.

"Are you kidding?" I replied. "We have to get back to the store. Mr. Kramer knows we didn't have a lot of deliveries. Besides..."

"Relax," Joel interrupted. "I mean, will you just trust me to work it out? I guarantee that it'll be okay."

He opened the door and got out, but I just sat there behind the steering wheel. Joel was always working the angles and so far he hadn't gotten caught. This was different, though. This time he was asking me to go along with him.

"Are you coming or not?" he demanded.

"I don't know," I answered. "It doesn't seem right.'"

"Don't be wound up so tight," he advised. "Or is having fun against your religion?"

For a second I nearly wished I hadn't opened my mouth to Joel about my faith, but I had. "I just believe in giving a guy his money's worth and Mr. Kramer isn't paying me to play."

"Kramer won't know anything about it," Joel hissed, leaning through the window on his side of the car. "What's the matter, can't you Christians do anything?"

That just about did it. The last thing I wanted was to give Joel a negative impression of being a Christian, but at the same time I wasn't quite dumb enough to give in. Still, I was tempted. "What'll we tell Mr. Kramer if we get back an hour late?"

Joel grinned. "We had a flat tire!"

"Yeah, but we didn't. Besides, he'll want to see a receipt if we got it repaired."

"We didn't get it repaired," Joel informed me. "We just put on the spare ourselves. We had some trouble with the jack, that's why it took so long. It's foolproof! Come on."

I knew I'd never get through to Joel if he thought Christianity was nothing but rules and regulations. I could make up the extra time at the warehouse later and he'd never know the difference. But something told me it was still wrong, regardless of how much rationalizing I did.

"I'm going back to work, Joel," I heard myself say.

"Don't be a jerk all your life," he began.

I answered him by starting the motor. I guess he knew I wasn't kidding, because he got in, slamming the door shut behind him. "I won't forget this, Turner," he snapped.

"You guys are back early," Rex Keller said as I parked the car. He ran the loading dock for Mr. Kramer.

"Yeah, we are." Joel agreed, giving me a nasty look.

"It was a light load," I added, ignoring Joel.

"We can use some help inside," Rex went on.

"Thanks to you, we'll be working in that hot warehouse all afternoon when we could be at Harry's," Joel hissed.

Joel wasn't kidding about the warehouse. It was like an oven, with little ventilation. Admittedly I had second thoughts about my decision as perspiration started running off my body a few minutes later. Joel kept his distance too, working at the other end of the building. Up until that day we had gotten along pretty well, despite our differences.

"Joel, Sam, I'd like to see you in the office," Mr. Kramer announced suddenly. It was cool in his office. I could have sat there for the rest of the day! "Was there some reason why you didn't turn in your routing sheet, Joel?" Mr. Kramer asked.

Joel gave me a superior, amused look. "Sam was in charge of the paperwork today," he replied.

"Oh no!" I groaned. "Left it in the car! Be right back." I stood up and headed for the door.

"You can get it later," Mr. Kramer assured me. "Have a seat, Sam. I really called you in here to commend you for the work you've both been doing lately. I've gotten nothing but good reports from customers for your fast, courteous service."

"Thanks a lot," I said.

"Yeah, thanks," Joel added.

"A job of this type requires men who are trustworthy," Mr. Kramer continued. "Once you leave the store you're pretty much on your own. Unfortunately not everyone can handle this kind of freedom and I was admittedly apprehensive about hiring guys your age." Joel and I just sat there.

"No more," Mr. Kramer went on. "I now have total confidence in you. I hope you'll both be with us for a long time."

"Fine with me," Joel replied.

"Me too," I agreed, "except it'll have to be part-time when school starts."

"Yes, I understand that," Mr. Kramer answered. "In fact, your honesty when you applied was one reason I hired you."

"Oh, he's real honest," Joel said, giving me a look. Naturally Mr. Kramer didn't catch the sarcasm.

"I'll let you get back to work now," Mr. Kramer decided. "By the way, did you have any trouble with the car, Sam?"

I frowned. "Trouble? No, none at all."

"Good. After you left, I remembered that the car you took doesn't have a spare tire," Mr. Kramer explained. "We'll see that it doesn't happen again."

Joel swallowed. "No spare."

"I'm just glad you didn't have a flat," Mr. Kramer said with a smile. "That'll be all. Oh, let me have that routing sheet as soon as possible, Sam."

"Yes, sir," I agreed, quickly leaving the office. Joel was right behind me, though.

"Hey, Sam, wait up!" he whispered.

"Have to get that routing sheet," I replied, trying hard not to laugh.

"Did you know we didn't have a spare?" Joel wanted to know.

"No, of course not," I answered truthfully.

"Oh man, if I had told Kramer we had a flat and changed it ourselves...."

"But you didn't," I reminded him. "I'd better get that routing sheet."

I hurried on to the parking lot, grinning all the way. Joel and his fool-proof scheme! If I had given into temptation and gone along with it I would have been the fool. An unemployed one.

The Toolbox

JOSHUA HARRIS
FROM *I KISSED DATING GOODBYE*

Recently my dad and my younger brother Joel attended a birthday party for Stephen Taylor, one of Joel's best friends. It was a very special occasion. Stephen was turning thirteen, and his dad wanted to make Stephen's entrance into young adulthood memorable. Nice presents wouldn't suffice; Stephen's dad wanted to impart wisdom. To accomplish this he asked fathers to accompany their sons to the party and to bring a special gift—a tool that served them in their specific lines of work.

Each father gave his tool to Stephen along with its accompanying "life lesson" for the "toolbox" of principles Stephen would carry into life. The tools were as unique as the men who used them. My dad gave Stephen a quality writing pen and explained that a pen not only served him when he wrote his ideas but also represented his word when he signed an agreement.

During the gift giving, a father who was a professional home builder handed Stephen a small box. "Inside that box is the tool I use most," he said. Stephen opened it and found a nail puller.

"My nail puller, simple as it might seem," the father explained, "is one of the most important tools I have." This father told the story of how once, while in the middle of building a wall, he discovered that it was crooked. Instead of halting the construction and undoing a little work to fix the wall, he decided to proceed, hoping that the problem would go away as he continued to build. However, the problem only worsened. Eventually, at a great loss of materials and time, he had to tear down the nearly completed wall and totally rebuild it.

"Stephen," the father said gravely, "times will come in life when you'll realize you've made a mistake. At that moment, you have two choices: You can swallow your pride and 'pull a few nails,' or you can foolishly continue your course, hoping the problem will go away. Most of the time the problem will only get worse. I'm giving you this tool to remind you of this principle: When you realize you've made a mistake, the best thing you can do is tear it down and start over."

The Joy Ride

SUZY RYAN

Growing up, I worshiped my father. Since my parents bitterly divorced when I was four years old, I did not see Dad much. My visits with him consisted of every other weekend, and some of my summer vacation. When I spent time with him, however, he did something that forever shaped my character. He validated me by listening to me, thus giving me confidence that my words were important.

Sunday nights, when Dad and I drove the hour to my house, we discussed politics, current events, and sports. He treated me like a young woman with worthwhile opinions.

At fourteen years old, I remember one car ride cringing in silence, because of what I needed to tell him.

Would Dad be mad? Would he think less of me? I held my breath and spilled out my story.

Earlier that week, I had spent the night at my friend Judy's house. As a freshman in high school, an "overnight" included baking a cake, playing cards, and watching TV. By midnight, we were bored. That is when her sixteen-year-old brother, Steve, walked in the door.

"Hey you guys—let's go for a joy ride," Judy suggested. "Mom and Dad are asleep, and we'll only drive down the street."

"No, Judy," I said. "You don't have a license, your parents would kill you, and besides, I'm tired and want to go to bed."

"Suzy, you're such a goody-goody," Judy complained. "Come on, loosen up! Don't ruin everyone's fun. I'll be waiting in Dad's truck."

Judy is right, I thought. *I am always afraid of getting into trouble. Maybe I should be more carefree like her. I really want her to like me. Oh well, what's the harm if Steve goes with us?*

Quickly, Steve and I piled into the Ford, as Judy revved the engine. Music blaring, we shot out of the driveway and started down the endless gravel road.

Since Judy lived out in the country, blackness blanketed the horizon. *This is fun! I'm glad I came and didn't mess up everyone's good time.* I sat between Steve and Judy, and of course, we wore no seat belts—we were invincible! Judy drove about forty-five miles per hour, and with a manic laugh, made a sharp turn to the left.

"Weeeeeee," she squealed, as gravel pinged like popcorn against the bottom of the vehicle. Judy careened the truck through the rock pile by the side of the road and then overcompensated with a sharp right to navigate back to the center. Unfortunately, the truck swerved too far right, blazing through another rock pile by the side of the road.

POP! BAM! POP! The gravel beat mercilessly against the bottom of the truck. Judy abruptly turned left, and then the truck's steering wheel started spinning wildly like a carnival ride. We helplessly spiraled from the left gravel pile to the right one. The car was desperately out of control. All of the sudden, Judy started screaming and took her hands off the wheel to cover her face. In vain, I grabbed the steering wheel trying to make it stop circling.

"Hit the brakes!" Steve screamed. Time ceased as we sailed through the air and crashed to the ground. While the truck continued to roll over and over, a floating sensation engulfed me and I thought, *Is this what it's like to die?*

This roller coaster nightmare tangled our bodies together like a deck of shuffled cards as we tumbled in the tiny cab and finally came to a halt in the ditch.

A deafening crash shattered my fog, and I struggled to break free from the arms, legs, and glass that smothered me. Somehow Steve opened the door, and I saw that the wreck had smashed the truck hood like a tin can.

Stunned, we scrambled like caged mice out of the totaled truck— without even a scratch.

That is when Judy took off running and said, "I'm going to kill myself! I'll be dead anyway when Dad finds out what's happened." Steve and I raced after her, and brought her back to the wreck. Although barefoot, we decided to sprint the two miles back to their house. I never felt a rock or a pebble, and never felt out of breath.

I had an overwhelming sensation that God had spared my life.

I calmly told my dad the story, and he listened to me without comment. I told him I was sorry and ashamed of myself. "I wanted Judy to like me," I confessed. "Usually I try to do the right thing, but I didn't want Judy to be mad at me. I've learned my lesson, Dad. I know I shouldn't have gone with her! I was wrong. Are you mad?"

Dad didn't say anything; he just looked at me with watery eyes. Finally he said, "Suzy, I'm just relieved that you're okay. You are a smart girl who made a mistake. I know you won't make it again."

Dad later told me, "I didn't have the heart to discipline you, because you were so hard on yourself."

At that moment, I determined not to let someone else drag me into a situation that I knew was wrong. Dad never mentioned the incident again, and he continued to talk to me like an adult with a keen mind. To this day, I know my zest for knowledge was spawned from a father who believed his daughter had something worthwhile to say, and was always ready to listen. Even when I made mistakes.

Making Sarah Cry

CHERYL L. COSTELLO-FORSHEY

He stood among his friends from school,
He joined their childhood games—
Laughing as they played kickball
And when they called poor Sarah names.
Sarah was unlike the rest;
She was slow and not as smart,
And it would seem to all his friends
She was born without a heart.
And so he gladly joined their fun
Of making Sarah cry.
But somewhere deep within his heart,
He never knew just why.
For he could hear his mother's voice,
Her lessons of right and wrong
Playing over and over inside his head
Just like a favorite song.

"Treat others with respect, son,
The way you'd want them treating you.
And remember, when you hurt others,
Someday, someone might hurt you."
He knew his mother wouldn't understand
The purpose of their game
Of teasing Sarah, who made them laugh
As her own tears fell like rain.
The funny faces that she made
And the way she'd stomp her feet
Whenever they mocked the way she walked
Or the stutter when she'd speak.
To him she must deserve it
Because she never tried to hide.
And if she truly wanted to be left alone,
Then she should stay inside.
But every day she'd do the same:
She'd come outside to play,
And stand there, tears upon her face,
Too upset to run away.
The game would soon be over
As tears dropped from her eyes,
For the purpose of their fun
Was making Sarah cry.
It was nearly two whole months
He hadn't seen his friends.
He was certain they all must wonder

What happened and where he'd been
So he felt a little nervous
As he limped his way to class.
He hoped no one would notice,
He prayed no one would ask
About that awful day:
The day his bike met with a car,
Leaving him with a dreadful limp
And a jagged-looking scar.
So he held his breath a little
As he hobbled into the room,
Where inside he saw a "Welcome Back" banner
And lots of red balloons.
He felt a smile cross his face
As his friends all smiled, too,
And he couldn't wait to play outside—
His favorite thing to do.
So the second that he stepped outdoors
And saw his friends all waiting there,
He expected a few pats on the back—
Instead, they all stood back and stared.
He felt his face grow hotter
As he limped to join their side
To play a game of kickball
And of making Sarah cry.
An awkward smile crossed his face
When he heard somebody laugh

And heard the words, "Hey freak,
Where'd you get the ugly mask?"
He turned, expecting Sarah,
But Sarah could not be seen.
It was the scar upon his own face
That caused such words so mean.
He joined in their growing laughter,
Trying hard to not give in
To the awful urge inside to cry
Or the quivering of his chin.
They are only teasing,
He made himself believe.
They are still my friends;
They'd never think of hurting me.
But the cruel remarks continued
About the scar and then his limp.
And he knew if he shed a single tear
They'd label him a wimp.
And so the hurtful words went on,
And in his heart he wondered why.
But he knew without a doubt
The game would never end, until they made him cry.
And just when a tear had formed,
He heard a voice speak out from behind.
"Leave him alone you bullies,
Because he's a friend of mine."
He turned to see poor Sarah,

Determination on her face,
Sticking up for one of her own tormentors
And willing to take his place.
And when his friends did just that,
Trying their best to make poor Sarah cry,
This time he didn't join in,
And at last understood exactly why.
"Treat others with respect, son,
The way you'd want them treating you.
And remember, when you hurt others,
Someday, someone might hurt you."
It took a lot of courage
But he knew he must be strong,
For at last he saw the difference
Between what's right and wrong.
And Sarah didn't seem so weird
Through his understanding eyes.
Now he knew he'd never play again
The game of making Sarah cry.
It took several days of teasing
And razzing from his friends,
But when they saw his strength,
They chose to be like him.
And now out on the playground,
A group of kids meets every day
For a game of kickball and laughter
And teaching their new friend, Sarah, how to play.

Changing

Things I've Learned Lately...

College might not be what I imagine,
Sometimes you have to let people go,
There is a time for everything,
And being challenged to grow is a good thing.

Eighth Grade Bully

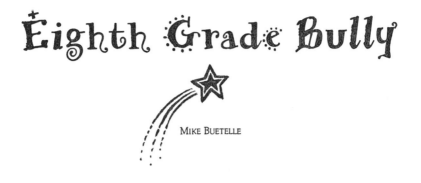

Mike Buetelle

hen I was in junior high, the eighth-grade bully punched me in the stomach. Not only did it hurt and make me angry, but the embarrassment and humiliation were almost intolerable. I wanted desperately to even the score! I planned to meet him by the bike racks the next day and let him have it.

For some reason, I told my plan to Nana, my grandmother—big mistake. She gave me one of her hour-long lectures (that woman could really talk). The lecture was a total drag, but among other things, I vaguely remember her telling me that I didn't need to worry about him. She said, "Good deeds beget good results, and evil deeds beget bad results." I told her, in a nice way, of course, that I thought she was full of it. I told her that I did good things all the time, and all I got in return was "baloney!" (I didn't use that word.) She stuck to her guns, though. She said, "Every good deed will come back to you someday, and every bad thing you do will also come back to you."

It took me thirty years to understand the wisdom of her words. Nana was living in a board-and-care home in Laguna Hills, California. Each Tuesday, I came by and took her out to dinner. I would always find her neatly dressed and sitting in a chair right by the front door. I vividly remember our very last dinner together before she went into the convalescent hospital. We drove to a nearby simple little family-owned restaurant. I ordered pot roast for Nana and a hamburger for myself. The food arrived and as I dug in, I noticed that Nana wasn't eating. She was just staring at the food on her plate. Moving my plate aside, I took Nana's plate, placed it in front of me and cut her meat into small pieces. I then placed the plate back in front of her. As she very weakly, and with great difficulty, forked the meat into her mouth, I was struck with a memory that brought instant tears to my eyes. Forty years previously, as a little boy sitting at the table, Nana had always taken the meat on my plate and cut it into small pieces so I could eat it.

It had taken forty years, but the good deed had been repaid. Nana was right. We reap exactly what we sow. "Every good deed you do will someday come back to you."

What about the eighth-grade bully?

He ran into the ninth-grade bully.

Wake-Up Call

BOB WELCH
FROM *A FATHER FOR ALL SEASONS*

was sitting in a bathtub full of moldy sheet rock when my thirteen-year-old son asked the question. "Can you take me golfing sometime?" he said.

I had a bathroom to remodel. It was fall, and the forecast for the next week was for one hundred percent chance of Oregon's liquid sunshine. I wanted to say no. "Sure," I said. "What did you have in mind?"

"Well, maybe you could, like, pick up Jared and me after school on Friday and take us out to Oakway."

"Sounds good."

Friday came. The showers continued. Looking out the window, moldy sheet rock seemed the saner choice. But at the appointed hour, I changed from home-improvement garb to rain-protection garb and loaded the boys' clubs and mine in the back of the car. In front of the school, Ryan and Jared piled in. Ryan looked at me with a perplexed expression.

"What's with the golf hat, Dad?" he said.

It was, I thought, a silly question, like asking a scuba diver what's with the swim fins.

"Well, I thought we were going to play some golf."

A peculiar pause ensued, like a phone line temporarily gone dead.

"Uh, you're going, too?" he asked.

Suddenly, it struck me like a three-iron to my gut: I hadn't been invited.

Thirteen years of parenting flashed before my eyes. The birth. The diapers. The late-night feedings. Helping with homework. Building forts. Fixing bikes. Going to games. Going camping. Going everywhere together—my son and I.

Now I hadn't been invited. This was it. This was the end of our relationship as I had always known it. This was "Adios, Old Man, thanks for the memories but I'm old enough to swing my own clubs now, so go back to your rocking chair and crossword puzzles and—oh yeah—here's a half-off coupon for your next bottle of Geritol."

All these memories sped by in about two seconds, leaving me about three seconds to respond before Ryan would get suspicious and think I had actually expected to be playing golf with him and his friend.

I had to say something. I wanted to say this: How could you do this to me? Throw me overboard like unused crab bait? We had always been a team. But this was abandonment. Adult abuse.

This was Lewis turning to Clark in 1805 and saying: "Later, Bill. I can make it the rest of the way to Oregon without you." John Glenn radioing Mission Control to say, thanks, but he could take it from here. Simon bailing out on Garfunkel during "Bridge Over Troubled Water."

Why did it all have to change?

Enough of this mind-wandering. I needed to level with him. I needed to express how hurt I was. Share my gut-level feelings. Muster all the courage I could find, bite the bullet, and spill my soul.

So I said, "Me? Play? Naw. You know I'm up to my ears in the remodel project."

We drove on in silence for a few moments. "So, how are you planning to pay for this?" I asked, my wounded ego reaching for the dagger.

"Uh, could you loan me seven dollars?"

Oh, I get it. He doesn't want me, but he'll gladly take my money.
"No problem," I said.

I dropped him and Jared off, wished them luck, and headed for home. My son was on his own now. Nobody there to tell him how to fade a five-iron, how to play that tricky downhiller, how to hit the sand shot. And what if there's lightning? What about hypothermia? A runaway golf cart? A band of militant gophers? He's so small. Who will take care of him?

There I was, alone, driving away from him. Not just for now. Forever. This was it. The bond was broken. Life would never be the same.

I walked in the door. "What are you doing home?" my wife asked.

I knew it would sound like some thirteen-year-old who was the only one in the gang not invited to the slumber party, but maintaining my immature demeanor, I said it anyway.

"I wasn't invited," I replied, with a trace of snottiness.

Another one of those peculiar pauses ensued. Then my wife laughed. Out loud. At first I was hurt. Then I, too, laughed, the situation suddenly becoming much clearer.

I went back to the bathroom remodel and began realizing that this is what life is all about: change. This is what father and sons must ultimately do: change. This is what I've been preparing him for since he first looked at me and screamed in terror: not to play golf without me, but to take on the world without me. With his own set of clubs. His own game plan. His own faith.

God was remodeling my son. Adding some space here. Putting in a new feature there. In short, allowing him to become more than he could ever be if I continued to hover over him. Just like when I was a kid and, at Ryan's age, I would sling my plaid golf bag over my shoulder and ride my bike five miles across town to play golf at a small public course called Marysville that I imagined as Augusta National.

I remember how grown-up I felt, walking into that dark clubhouse, the smoke rising from the poker game off to the left, and proudly pluncking down my two dollars for nine holes. Would I have wanted my father there with me that day? Naw. A boy's gotta do what a boy's gotta do: grow up.

I went back to the bathroom remodel project. A few hours later, I heard Ryan walk in the front door. I heard him complain to his mother that his putts wouldn't drop, that his drives were slicing, and that the course was like a lake. He sounded like someone I knew. His tennis shoes squeaked with water as I heard him walk back to where I was working on the bathroom.

"Dad," he said, dripping on the floor, "my game stinks. Can you take me golfing sometime? I need some help."

I wanted to hug him. Rev my radial-arm saw in celebration. Shout: "I'm still needed!" I wanted to tell God, "Thanks for letting me be part of this kid's remodel job."

Instead, I got one of those serious-dad looks on my face and stoically said, "Sure, Ry, anytime."

The Story Teller

AUTHOR UNKNOWN

A few months before I was born, my dad met a stranger who was new to our small Tennessee town. From the beginning, Daddy was fascinated with this enchanting newcomer and soon invited him to live with our family. The stranger was quickly accepted and was around to welcome me into the world a few months later.

As I grew up, I never questioned his place in our family. In my young mind, each member had a special niche. My brother, Bill, who was five years older than me, was my example. Fran, my younger sister, gave me an opportunity to play big brother and develop the art of teasing. My parents were complementary instructors—Mom taught me to love the Bible, and Dad taught me to obey it. But the stranger was our story teller. He could weave the most fascinating tales. Adventures, mysteries, and comedies were daily conversations. He could hold our whole family spellbound for hours each evening.

If I wanted to know about politics, history, or science, he knew it all. He knew about the past, understood the present, and seemingly could predict the future. The pictures he could draw were so lifelike that I would often laugh or cry as I watched.

He was like a friend to the whole family. He took Dad, Bill, and me to our first major league baseball game. He was always encouraging us to see the movies and he even made arrangements to introduce us to several movie stars. My brother and I were deeply impressed by John Wayne in particular.

The stranger was an incessant talker. Dad didn't seem to mind—but sometimes Mom would quietly get up while the rest of us were enthralled with one of his stories of faraway places—go to her room, read her Bible, and pray. I wonder now if she ever prayed that the stranger would leave. You see, my dad ruled our household with certain moral convictions. But this stranger never felt an obligation to honor them. Profanity, for example, was not allowed in our house—not from us, from our friends, or adults. Our longtime visitor, however, used occasional four letter words that burned my ears and made Dad squirm. To my knowledge, the stranger was never confronted. My dad didn't permit alcohol in his home—not even for cooking. But the stranger felt like we needed exposure and enlightened us to other ways of life. He offered us beer and other alcoholic beverages often.

He made cigarettes look tasty, cigars manly, and pipes distinguished. He talked freely, openly, and often about sex. His comments were sometimes blatant, sometimes suggestive, and generally embarrassing. I know now that my early concepts of the man/woman relationships were influenced by the stranger.

As I look back I believe it was the grace of God that the stranger did not influence us more. Time after time he opposed the values of my parents. Yet he was seldom rebuked and never asked to leave.

More than thirty years have passed since the stranger moved in with the young family on Morningside Drive. He is not nearly so intriguing to my dad as he was in those early years. But if I were to walk into my parents' den today, you would still see him sitting over in a corner, waiting for someone to listen to him talk and watch him draw his pictures.

His name?

We always just called him TV.

Full Circle

Janna L. Graber

From my bedroom I heard the sharp flip of a light switch, and then the thud of my father's footsteps in the hallway. I turned over in my bed and groaned, knowing exactly what his next words would be.

"It's 7:00. Time to wake up!" came his cheery voice.

I pulled the pillow over my head. "Can't I sleep in a little bit this morning?" I complained. After all, I thought, I was eighteen years old now.

"We've got chores to do," my dad replied in a voice that said I should know better. "Everyone's ready for breakfast already."

I grumbled as I got ready. *Why couldn't I live in a normal family?* I thought.

By the time I got downstairs, my family was already seated around the long oak table in our kitchen. My seven younger brothers and sisters, ranging from age sixteen down to age one, sat poised to pounce on the food as soon as the blessing was said.

With eight children, five of them adopted, my family was not the normal suburban household. To top it off, we lived in a farmhouse on a small acreage that was surrounded by the Denver suburbs. The idea of doing chores—feeding livestock, cleaning barns, and gardening—was foreign to my city friends. While they slept late or watched cartoons on Saturday mornings, I was doing chores with my family—something I was beginning to dislike.

Breakfast had been devoured by the time I finally turned to my dad. "What's the job today?" I asked, making it clear that I thought I should still be asleep in bed.

"The orchard," he replied. "It needs watering and weeding. If we work together, it'll be done in an hour."

The "orchard" was nothing more than twenty knee-high saplings. Two of my sisters pulled the hoses out to water, while Mom and Dad got down on their knees to weed. I grabbed a hose too, and halfheartedly pointed water on the trees struggling to survive in the dry Colorado soil.

"No, you've got to let it soak in," my father said as he walked over to inspect my work. "Keep the hose on them longer."

My frustration was hard to hide. "Why do we have to water these dumb sticks anyway? They'll never amount to anything!"

Dad looked at me evenly, as if considering a proper response. "These 'dumb sticks' will someday grow into beautiful trees. Your mom and I want a nice home for our family; it's a dream we have." He paused, and I saw his eyes scan our home, then turn to rest on my siblings. "Most dreams take hard work and time," he continued. "You need to keep that in mind."

With that, he went back to work, leaving me to consider his words. I looked at my family. Mom was helping two of my brothers pull weeds around the raspberry bushes, while a sister looked over the two youngest who were playing in the grass. My dad had chosen the hardest job of planting another young sapling in the hard clay earth.

I saw sweat on his brow as he toiled under the searing sun. Why, I wondered, did he do it? Why did he work so hard for us?

"Hey, Dad," my brother Philip called, "come look at my work!"

My dad walked over to Philip, who, at twelve, was struggling to fix a broken fence. Philip's work was clumsy, and bent nails protruded from the uneven slats he had replaced. But he beamed with pride as he showed off his handiwork.

I snickered. Couldn't Philip see that the job would need to be redone?

My dad's response surprised me. "Good job!" he said. "You went to it and got it done!"

The scene made me wonder. It would have been easier if Dad had done the job himself. What benefit was there for my brother to bungle through the work?

And why didn't we move into a house that required less upkeep? Did my parents enjoy all this work, or did they have another motive?

The home we lived in now looked nothing like when we had bought it. Built during the depression, the white farmhouse had consisted of two rooms and a tiny added-on kitchen. But my parents had seen the home's potential. They spent the next few years remodeling and landscaping. When the house got too small, they built on—three times— until the once-small farmhouse was a lovely home just right for raising eight children. I had never really thought about all my parents had done for us— until now.

I was quiet as I went back to my work, wondering about my parents and what they were trying to teach us.

Years have flown by since that day in the orchard, but I've thought a lot about my father's words. "Most dreams take hard work and time," he had said. "You need to keep that in mind."

Those sentiments echoed in my mind through college, a new career, and marriage. In fact, my father's words and example have become so engrained, that sometimes they begin to slip out.

When my husband and I purchased our first home, it was clear the place needed some work. The bare landscape needed attention, and I purchased dozens of flowers, bushes, and tiny trees.

A few days later, I invited my parents for a visit, and proudly showed them my purchases.

"Let's put them in," my mom said, as she headed to the garage for a shovel.

We eagerly planned and got to work. I took the shovel, and had begun to dig a hole when I stopped. There was something missing.

I ran inside the house, and found my two daughters who were watching a video with a friend.

"Come on outside and help," I called. "We can plant these trees together."

A surprised look came over their faces as I showed them how to hold the trees as I planted them.

"But these don't look like trees," my oldest exclaimed. "Why do we have to do this?"

My answer came without thinking. "If we do it together, the job goes much faster. Besides, they may not look like much now," I told her, "but with a little work and time, they'll grow into something beautiful."

Then, out of the corner of my eye, I saw my father grin.

My Own Rainbow

RANDI CURTISS
AGE 14
FROM *WHERE THE HEART IS*

Thanks to my family, I've learned that money isn't necessary for true happiness. My father is self-employed, and looking back I can see how much I didn't have. But the thought never even occurred to me at the time. I always thought of myself as the luckiest kid alive. I had a windmill not ten feet outside my front door, even though the well was dry and it creaked noisily whenever the wind blew. I had a back porch, even though it was only the size of a picnic table and covered with green, fake grass. I had the large herd of ducks and geese that Mom kept in a pen behind the trailer. We used to let them out, then stand on the back porch and toss bread. They'd race all over, stealing bits off each other's pieces.

And I had my rainbow. In the small bedroom where the three of us kids were crammed together, there was a small window with a clear rainbow sticker on it. I used to sit for hours, staring at the wind-tossed prairie grass through the red, orange, and yellow, and watching the clouds turn colors as they passed through the curved bands of color.

We eventually moved into a house not three hundred feet from where the trailer once stood, and I've never seen my rainbow since. Mom still has her poultry, but we took the windmill out because it was becoming dangerous to have around. I don't know what happened to the back porch.

We loaded the trailer onto a semi-truck bed one day, and I waved good-bye to my home of five years. Now all that's left of the trailer is the perimeter of blue irises that grew around it. But I'll never forget what I learned about happiness living there.

What Matters

No matter where you go or what you do,
or even what you try to achieve or master,
whatever you accomplish will not amount to anything without love.

—*Aubrey Leigh Denzer*
Graduation speech, Sisters High School

Curse or Blessing

MAX LUCADO
FROM *IN THE EYE OF THE STORM*

Once there was an old man who lived in a tiny village. Although poor, he was envied by all, for he owned a beautiful white horse. Even the king coveted his treasure. A horse like this had never been seen before—such was its splendor, its majesty, its strength.

People offered fabulous prices for the steed, but the old man always refused. "This horse is not a horse to me," he would tell them. "It is a person. How could you sell a person? He is a friend, not a possession. How could you sell a friend?" The man was poor and the temptation was great. But he never sold the horse.

One morning he found that the horse was not in the stable. All the village came to see him. "You old fool," they scoffed, "we told you that someone would steal your horse. We warned you that you would be robbed. You are so poor. How could you ever hope to protect such a valuable animal? It would have been better to have sold him. You could have gotten whatever price you wanted. No amount would have been too high. Now the horse is gone, and you've been cursed with misfortune."

The old man responded, "Don't speak too quickly. Say only that the horse is not in the stable. That is all we know; the rest is judgment. If I've been cursed or not, how can you know? How can you judge?"

The people contested, "Don't make us out to be fools! We may not be philosophers, but great philosophy is not needed. The simple fact that your horse is gone is a curse."

The old man spoke again. "All I know is that the stable is empty, and the horse is gone. The rest I don't know. Whether it be a curse or a blessing, I can't say. All we can see is a fragment. Who can say what will come next?"

The people of the village laughed. They thought that the man was crazy. They had always thought he was a fool; if he wasn't, he would have sold the horse and lived off the money. But instead, he was a poor woodcutter, an old man still cutting firewood and dragging it out of the forest and selling it. He lived hand to mouth in the misery of poverty. Now he had proven that he was, indeed, a fool.

After fifteen days, the horse returned. He hadn't been stolen; he had run away into the forest. Not only had he returned, he had brought a dozen wild horses with him. Once again the village people gathered around the wood-cutter and spoke. "Old man, you were right and we were wrong. What we thought was a curse was a blessing. Please forgive us."

The man responded, "Once again, you go too far. Say only that the horse is back. State only that a dozen horses returned with him, but don't judge. How do you know if this is a blessing or not? You see only a fragment. Unless you know the whole story, how can you judge? You read only one page of a book. Can you judge the whole book? You read only one word of a phrase. Can you understand the entire phrase?

"Life is so vast, yet you judge all of life with one page or one word. All you have is a fragment. Don't say that this is a blessing. No one knows. I am content with what I know. I am not perturbed by what I don't."

Maybe the old man is right, they said to one another. So they said little. But down deep, they knew he was wrong. They knew it was a blessing. Twelve wild horses had returned with one horse. With a little bit of work, the animals could be broken and trained and sold for much money.

The old man had a son, an only son. The young man began to break the wild horses. After a few days, he fell from one of the horses and broke both legs. Once again the villagers gathered around the old man and cast their judgments.

"You were right," they said. "You proved you were right. The dozen horses were not a blessing. They were a curse. Your only son has broken his legs, and now in your old age you have no one to help you. Now you are poorer than ever."

The old man spoke again. "You people are obsessed with judging. Don't go so far. Say only that my son broke his legs. Who knows if it is a blessing or a curse? No one knows. We only have a fragment. Life comes in fragments."

It so happened that a few weeks later the country engaged in war against a neighboring country. All the young men of the village were required to join the army. Only the son of the old man was excluded, because he was injured. Once again the people gathered around the old man, crying and screaming because their sons had been taken. There was little chance that they would return. The enemy was strong, and the war would be a losing struggle. They would never see their sons again.

"You were right, old man," they wept. "God knows you were right. This proves it. Your son's accident was a blessing. His legs may be broken, but at least he is with you. Our sons are gone forever."

The old man spoke again. "It is impossible to talk with you. You always draw conclusions. No one knows. Say only this: Your sons had to go to war, and mine did not. No one knows if it is a blessing or a curse. No one is wise enough to know. Only God knows."

She's Seventeen

GLORIA GAITHER
FROM *LET'S MAKE A MEMORY*

The first day of school didn't start until one o'clock, so there was plenty of time for breakfast at McDonald's and shopping for the supplies that had been listed in the *Times-Tribune* the Wednesday before. You reminded us to go to McDonald's for breakfast. "We've always gone there on the first day of school," you said. Something hard to label stirred inside me when you said it. Perhaps it was pride—pride that you still found joy in our crazy little tradition; or perhaps it was pleasure—pleasure in knowing that you still choose to be with our family when you have your "druthers." But there was a certain sadness, too, and I couldn't stop the knowing this was your last first day of school.

You came down the stairs that morning all neat and well-groomed, the healthy glow of your summer tan and freckles still showing through your make-up, your sun-bleached hair carefully arranged. "Hi, Mom!" you said, and your grin showed your straight, white teeth. No more orthodontist appointments, I thought, and no more broken glasses to glue before school. Contacts and braces had sure been worth it.

"I've got to have my senior pictures taken tomorrow after school, Mom. Can I use the car?"

"As far as I know," I answered, then reminded you of your promise to take your sister to get her hair trimmed at three o'clock that afternoon. Your driver's license had come in handy, too.

By then Amy and Benjy were ready, and we all piled into the car and drove to McDonald's. As we ate, we talked about other first days—the first day of kindergarten, their first day of junior high, and that scary first day in the big new high school. You all interrupted each other with stories of embarrassing moments, awards, friendships, and fright.

After we had eaten, we hurried to buy notebook paper and compasses before I dropped you all at school—first Amy and Benjy at the middle school, then you. "Bye, Mom," you said as you scooted across the seat. Then you stopped a moment and looked back over your shoulder. "And, Mom...thanks." It was the remnant of a kiss good-bye. It was the hesitancy of a little girl in ringlets beginning kindergarten. It was the anticipation of a young woman confident of her direction—these were all there in that gesture.

"I love you," was all I answered, but I had hoped that somehow you could hear with your heart the rest of the words that were going through my mind—words that told you how special you are to us; words that would let you know how rich your father and I have been because you came into our lives; words that tell you how much we believe in you, hope for you, pray for you, thank God for you. As the school doors closed behind you and you disappeared into the corridor, I wanted so to holler after you: "Wait! We have so much yet to do. We've never been to Hawaii. We've never taken a cruise. That book of poetry we wrote together isn't published yet. And what about the day we were going to spend at the cabin just being still and reading? Or the writers' workshop we planned to attend together in Illinois? You can't go yet.... WAIT!"

But I knew you couldn't wait, and that we could never keep you by calling a halt to your progress. You had promises to keep. And so, though I knew this was a last first, I also somehow knew that it was a first in a whole lifetime of new beginnings...and I rejoiced!

Dad

AUTHOR UNKNOWN

4 years:	My daddy can do anything.
7 years:	My dad knows a lot, a whole lot.
8 years:	My father doesn't know quite everything.
12 years:	Oh, well, naturally Father doesn't know that, either.
14 years:	Father? Hopelessly old-fashioned.
21 years:	Oh, that man is out-of-date. What did you expect?
25 years:	He knows a little bit about it, but not much.
30 years:	Maybe we ought to find out what Dad thinks.
35 years:	A little patience. Let's get Dad's assessment before we do anything.
50 years:	I wonder what Dad would have thought about that. He was pretty smart.
60 years:	My dad knew absolutely everything!
65 years:	I'd give anything if Dad were here so I could talk this over with him. I really miss that man.

The Signal

RETOLD BY ALICE GRAY

The young man sat alone on the bus and most of the time stared out the window. He was in his mid-twenties, nice looking with a kind face. His dark blue shirt matched the color of his eyes. His hair was short and neat. Occasionally he would look away from the window and the anxiety on his young face touched the heart of the grandmotherly woman sitting across the aisle. The bus was just approaching the outskirts of a small town when she was so drawn to the young man that she scooted across the aisle and asked permission to sit next to him.

After a few moments of small talk about the warm spring weather, he blurted out, "I've been in prison for two years. I just got out this morning and I'm going home." His words tumbled out as he told her he was raised in a poor but proud family and how his crime had brought his family shame and heartbreak. In the whole two years he had not heard from them. He knew they were too poor to travel the distance to where he had been in prison and his parents probably felt too uneducated to write. He had stopped writing them when no answers came.

Three weeks before being released, he desperately wrote one more letter to his family. He told them how sorry he was for disappointing them and asked for their forgiveness.

He went on to explain about being released from prison and that he would take the bus to his hometown—the one that goes right by the front yard of the house where he grew up and where his parents still lived. In his letter, he said he would understand if they wouldn't forgive him.

He wanted to make it easy for them and so asked them to give him a signal that he could see from the bus. If they had forgiven him and wanted him to come back home, they could tie a white ribbon on the old apple tree that stood in the front yard. If the signal wasn't there, he would stay on the bus, leave town, and be out of their lives forever.

As the bus neared his street, the young man became more and more anxious to the point he was afraid to look out the window because he was so sure there would be no ribbon.

After listening to his story, the woman asked simply, "Would it help if we traded seats and I'll sit near to the window and look for you?" The bus traveled a few more blocks and then she saw the tree. She gently touched the young man's shoulder and choking back tears said, "Look! Oh look! The whole tree is covered with white ribbons."

The Riddle

AUTHOR UNKNOWN

I am your constant companion.

I am your greatest helper or heaviest burden.

I will push you onward or drag you down to failure.

I am completely at your command.

Half the things you do might just as well be turned

over to me and I will be able to do them quickly and correctly.

I am easily managed—you must merely be firm with me.

Show me exactly how you want something done

and after a few lessons I will do it automatically.

I am the servant of all great people and, alas, of all failures, as well.

Those who are great, I have made great.

Those who are failures, I have made failures.

I am not a machine, though I work with all the precision

of a machine plus the intelligence of a person.

You may run me for profit or run me for ruin—it makes no difference to me.

Take me, train me, be firm with me,

and I will place the world at your feet.

Be easy with me and I will destroy you.

Who am I?

I am habit!

Life is no brief candle to me.
It is a sort of splendid torch which
I have got a hold of for a moment,
And I want to make it burn as brightly as possible
before handing it on to future generations.

—*George Bernard Shaw*

✤ Blue Ribbon

AUTHOR UNKNOWN

Who You Are Makes a Difference...

A teacher in New York decided to honor each of her seniors in high school by telling them the difference they each made. She called each student to the front of the class, one at a time. First she told them how the student made a difference to her and the class. Then she presented each of them with a blue ribbon with gold letters which read, "Who I Am Makes a Difference."

Afterward the teacher decided to do a class project to see what kind of impact recognition would have on a community. She gave each of the students three more ribbons and instructed them to go out and spread this acknowledgment ceremony. Then they were to follow up on the results, see who honored whom, and report back to the class in about a week.

One of the boys in the class went to a junior executive in a nearby company and honored him for helping him with his career planning. He gave him a blue ribbon and put it on his shirt. Then he gave him two extra ribbons, and said, "We're doing a class project on recognition, and we'd like you to go out, find somebody to honor, give them a blue ribbon, then give them the extra blue ribbon so they can acknowledge a third person to keep this acknowledgment ceremony going. Then please report back to me and tell me what happened."

Later that day the junior executive went in to see his boss, who had been noted, by the way, as being kind of a grouchy fellow. He sat his boss down and he told him that he deeply admired him for being a creative genius. The boss seemed very surprised. The junior executive asked him if he would accept the gift of the blue ribbon and would he give him permission to put it on him. His surprised boss said, "Well, sure."

The junior executive took the blue ribbon and placed it right on his boss's jacket above his heart. As he gave him the last extra ribbon, he said, "Would you do me a favor? Would you take this extra ribbon and pass it on by honoring somebody else? The young boy who first gave me the ribbons is doing a project in school and we want to keep this recognition ceremony going and find out how it affects people."

That night the boss came home to his fourteen-year-old son and sat him down. He said, "The most incredible thing happened to me today. I was in my office and one of the junior executives came in and told me he admired me and gave me a blue ribbon for being a creative genius. Imagine. He thinks I'm a creative genius. Then he put this blue ribbon that says 'Who I Am Makes A Difference' on my jacket above my heart. He gave me an extra ribbon and asked me to find somebody else to honor. As I was driving home tonight, I started thinking about whom I would honor with this ribbon and I thought about you. I want to honor you. My days are really hectic and when I come home I don't pay a lot of attention to you. Sometimes I scream at you for not getting enough good grades in school and for your bedroom being a mess, but somehow tonight, I just wanted to sit here and, well…just let you know that you do make a difference to me. Besides your mother, you are the most important person in my life. You're a great son, and I love you!"

The startled boy started to sob and sob, and he couldn't stop crying. His whole body shook. He looked up at his father and said through his tears, "Dad, I didn't think it mattered to you whether I lived or died. Now I know it does."

When one door closes, another opens.
But we often look so regretfully upon the closed door
That we don't see the one that has opened for us.

—Alexander Graham Bell

Choices

GRADUATION SPEECH
SARA ANN ZINN
CROOK COUNTY CHRISTIAN SCHOOL

*A*s graduating seniors we are faced with choices. Now is the time that we who once were children begin making decisions as adults.

The solid foundation of our Christian education and the forming of our beliefs and our character by this school and our families have prepared us for the journey ahead.

Some of us have already chosen the avenue that will lead to our goals and dreams—others are still at the crossroads. Some will go to college, some will get married and start families, some will go off to defend our nation, while others will immediately enter the workforce. Whatever choices we make, we must always remember who we are and what we represent.

The road is long, and the journey is rough
At times it seems hard to find strength enough.
But through it all, the ups and downs

CHANGING

We learn to smile despite the frowns.
We learn to share our joy and pain,
To share without expecting gain.
We learn to give a helping hand
And how to lean when we can't stand.
We learn the difference between right and wrong
To stand for right, and always stand strong.
Though this road is hard and seems so long
It's how we find where we belong;
Because it's only through life's bends and turns
That we can truly grow and truly learn.

Best Friends

Alicia M. Boxler

When I first met Molly, she instantly became my best friend. We enjoyed the same things, laughed at the same jokes, and even had the same love for sunflowers.

It seemed like we had found each other at the right time. Both of us had been in different groups of friends that didn't get along or we didn't feel comfortable in. We were thrilled to find each other.

Our friendship grew very strong. Our families became friends, and everyone knew that wherever you found Molly, you found me, and vice versa. In fifth grade, we were not in the same class, but at lunch we both sat in nearby assigned seats and turned around to talk to each other. The lunch ladies did not like this. We were always blocking the aisle, talking too loudly, and not eating our lunches, but we didn't care. The teachers knew we were best friends, but we were also a disturbance. Our big mouths got us into trouble, and we were warned that we would never be in the same classes again if we kept this up.

That summer, Molly and her brother were at my house quite often.

My mom took care of them while their mom worked. We went swimming, played outside, and practiced playing our flutes. We bought best friend charms and made sure to wear them as often as possible.

Summer went by very quickly, and middle school began. As the teachers had warned us, we were not in the same classes. We still talked on the phone, went over to each other's houses, sang in choir, and practiced our flutes together in band. Nothing could destroy this friendship.

Seventh grade started and, again, we were not in the same classes and could not sit near each other at lunch. It seemed as if we were being put to a test. We both made new friends. Molly started to hang out with a new group of people and was growing very popular.

We spent less time together, and we rarely talked on the phone. At school, I would try to talk to her, but she would just ignore me. When we did take a minute to talk, one of her more popular friends would come up and Molly would just walk away with her, leaving me in the dust. It hurt.

I was so confused. I'm sure she didn't know at the time how bad I felt, but how could I talk to her if she wouldn't listen? I began to hang around with my new friends, but it just wasn't the same. I met Erin, who was also a friend of Molly's. She was in the same situation I was with Molly. She and Molly had been close friends, and lately Molly had been treating Erin the same way as me. We decided to talk to her.

The phone call was not easy. Talking and saying how I felt was difficult. I was so afraid that I would hurt her feelings and make her angry. It was funny, though—when it was just the two of us talking on the phone, we were friends again. It was the old Molly.

I explained how I was feeling, and she did, too. I realized I was not the only one hurting. She was alone without me to talk to. What was she supposed to do, not make new friends? I didn't think about this before, but she was feeling left out by me and my new friends. There were times when I didn't even notice I was ignoring her. We must have talked for a long time, because once we were finished I had used a handful of tissues for my tears, and felt as if I had lifted a heavy weight off my heart. We both decided that we wanted to be with our new friends, but we would never forget the fun and friendship we had shared with each other.

Today, I look back on all of this and smile. Molly and I are finally in the same classes, and you know what? We still get in trouble for talking too loudly. Molly is not my best friend anymore, but more like my sister. We still enjoy the same things, laugh at the same jokes, and share the same love for sunflowers. I will never forget her. Molly taught me something very important. She taught me that things change, people change, and it doesn't mean you forget the past or try to cover it up. It simply means that you move on and treasure all the memories.

Faith

Things I've Learned Lately...

Some people are afraid to cry,
Heaven's got to be something special,
Coincidences are really "God-things,"
And love always trusts, always hopes

Kevin's Different World

KELLY ADKINS
FROM *CAMPUS LIFE* MAGAZINE

y brother Kevin thinks God lives under his bed. At least that's what I heard him say one night. He was praying out loud in his dark bedroom, and I stopped outside his closed door to listen.

"Are you there, God?" he said. "Where are you? Oh, I see. Under the bed."

I giggled softly and tiptoed off to my own room. Kevin's unique perspectives are often a source of amusement. But that night something else lingered long after the humor. I realized for the first time the very different world Kevin lives in.

He was born thirty years ago, mentally disabled as a result of difficulties during labor. Apart from his size (he's six-foot-two), there are few ways in which he is an adult. He reasons and communicates with the capabilities of a seven-year-old, and he always will.

He will probably always believe that God lives under his bed, that Santa Claus is the one who fills the space under our tree every Christmas, and that airplanes stay up in the sky because angels carry them.

I remember wondering if Kevin realizes he is different. Is he ever dissatisfied with his monotonous life? Up before dawn each day, off to work at a workshop for the disabled, home to walk our cocker spaniel, returning to eat his favorite macaroni and cheese for dinner, and later to bed. The only variation in the entire scheme are laundry days, when he hovers excitedly over the washing machine like a mother with her newborn child.

He does not seem dissatisfied. He lopes out to the bus every morning at 7:05, eager for a day of simple work. He wrings his hands excitedly while the water boils on the stove for dinner, and he stays up late twice a week to gather our dirty laundry for his next day's laundry chores.

And Saturdays—oh, the bliss of Saturdays! That's the day my dad takes Kevin to the airport to have a soft drink, watch the planes land, and speculate loudly on the destination of each passenger inside.

"That one's goin' to Chi-car-go!" Kevin shouts as he claps his hands. His anticipation is so great he can hardly sleep on Friday nights.

I don't think Kevin knows anything exists outside his world of daily rituals and weekend field trips. He doesn't know what it means to be discontent. His life is simple. He will never know the entanglement of wealth or power, and he does not care what brand of clothing he wears or what kind of food he eats. He recognizes no differences in people, treating each person as an equal and a friend. His needs have always been met, and he never worries that one day they may not be.

His hands are diligent. Kevin is never so happy as when he is working. When he unloads the dishwasher or vacuums the carpet, his heart is completely in it. He does not shrink from a job when it is begun, and he does not leave a job until it is finished. But when his tasks are done, Kevin knows how to relax. He is not obsessed with his work or the work of others.

His heart is pure. He still believes everyone tells the truth, promises must be kept, and when you are wrong, you apologize instead of argue. Free from pride and unconcerned with appearances, Kevin is not afraid to cry when he is hurt, angry, or sorry. He is always transparent, always sincere.

And he trusts God. Not confined by intellectual reasoning, when he comes to Christ, he comes as a child.

Kevin seems to know God—to really be friends with him—in a way that is difficult for an "educated" person to grasp. God seems like his closest companion.

In my moments of doubt and frustrations with my Christianity, I envy the security Kevin has in his simple faith. It is then that I am most willing to admit that he has some divine knowledge that rises above my mortal questions. It is then I realize that perhaps he is not the one with the handicap—I am.

One day, when the mysteries of heaven are opened, and we are all amazed at how close God really is to our hearts, I'll realize that God heard the simple prayers of a boy who believed that God lived under his bed.

Kevin won't be surprised at all.

How Sweet the Sound

CYNTHIA HAMOND

The lead should have been mine. All my friends agreed with me. At least, it shouldn't have been Helen's, that strange new girl. She never had a word to say, always looking down at her feet as if her life was too heavy anyway. We've never done anything to her. We think she's just stuck up. Things can't be all that bad for her, not with all the great clothes she wears. She hasn't worn the same thing more than twice in the two months she's been at our school.

But the worst of it was when she showed up at our tryouts and sang for my part. Everyone knew the lead role was meant for me. After all, I had parts in all our school musicals and this was our senior year.

My friends were waiting for me so I didn't hang around for Helen's audition. The shock came two days later when we hurried to check the drama department's bulletin board for the play postings

We scanned the sheets looking for my name. When we found it, I burst out in tears. Helen was slated to play the lead! I was to be her mother and her understudy. Understudy? Nobody could believe it.

Rehearsals seemed to go on forever. Helen didn't seem to notice that we were going out of our way to ignore her.

I'll admit it, Helen did have a beautiful voice. She was different on stage somehow. Not so much happy as settled and content.

Opening night had all its jitters. Everyone was quietly bustling around backstage waiting for the curtain to go up. Everyone but Helen, of course. She seemed contained in her own calm world.

The performance was a hit. Our timing was perfect, our voices blended and soared. Helen and I flowed back and forth, weaving the story between us. I the ailing mother praying for her wayward daughter and Helen playing the daughter who realizes as her mother dies that there is more to this life than *this* life.

The final scene reached its dramatic end. I was laying in the darkened bedroom. The prop bed I was on was uncomfortable, making it hard to stay still. I was impatient, anxious for Helen's big finish to be over.

She was spotlighted upstage, the grieving daughter beginning to understand the true meaning of the hymn she had been singing as her mother passed away.

"Amazing grace, how sweet the sound…" Her voice lifted over the pain of her mother's death and the joy of God's promises.

"…that saved a wretch like me.…" Something real was happening to me as Helen sang. My impatience left.

"…I once was lost but now I am found…" My heart was touched to tears.

"…was blind but now I see." My spirit began to turn within me and I turned to God. In that moment, I knew His love, His desire for me.

Helen's voice lingered in the prayer of the last note. The curtain dropped.

Complete silence. Not a sound. Helen stood behind the closed curtain, head bowed, gently weeping.

Suddenly applause and cheers erupted and when the curtain parted, Helen saw her standing ovation.

We all made our final bows. My hugs were genuine. My heart had been opened to the Great Love.

Then it was over. The costumes were hung up, makeup tissued off, the lights dimmed. Everyone went off in their usual groupings, congratulating each other.

Everyone but Helen. And everyone but me.

"Helen, your song, it was so real for me." I hesitated, my feelings intense. "You sang me into the heart of God."

Helen gasped. Her eyes met mine.

"That's what my mother said to me the night she died." A tear slipped down her cheek. My heart leapt to hers. "My mother was in such pain. Singing 'Amazing Grace' always comforted her. She said I should always remember that God has promised good to me and that His grace would lead her home."

Her face lit from the inside out, her mother's love shining through. "Just before she died she whispered, 'Sing me into the heart of God, Helen.' That night and tonight, I sang for my mother."

The Bullet

DORIS SANFORD

t was a late March afternoon and Anya sat in the car memorizing Bible verses. She did it every week while her little brother, Zeek, had his piano lesson. Her turn would come next, but memorizing meant repeating the verses out loud and that worked best in the car. She was a part of her junior high Bible Quiz team and that required knowing a part of one of the books of the Bible very well. No problem. Anya loved the competition!

Their music teacher lived in a two-story house and the piano was upstairs. Just before the lesson began, Zeek told his mom, "I want Sissy to listen to my lesson." Mom reminded him that Anya needed the study time, and besides, she had been listening to him practice his piano lesson all week at home. But Zeek was determined, he went down to the car and to Mom's surprise returned with his big sister in tow.

The lesson began. Five minutes later the lesson was abruptly halted by a loud noise outside. Everyone stopped to watch a late-model car speeding away. The lesson resumed after the teacher reassured them that it was probably the car's backfire they had heard.

Zeek's hands were barely on the piano when the teacher's husband rushed in: "A gun shot...into the car...shattered the passenger side window in the front seat!" The lesson was over. They hurried down to look. Sure enough, there was the bullet lodged in the backrest just where Anya's head had been five minutes earlier.

They all knew it immediately. God had used seven-year-old Zeek to save his sister's life. It was a profound moment. Zeek had responded when it hadn't made sense to him or anyone else, and Anya had complied with his illogical request.

The two snipers who were driving through the streets of Salem, Oregon, randomly shooting at mailboxes, cars, and houses, were arrested and held on one-million dollar bail. The district attorney asked Anya and Zeek to come to court and tell their story. The young men were sent to prison for five years, but not without hearing how God had protected a seven-year-old and his big sister.

Shark Attack!

RICK BUNDSCHUH
FROM *BREAKAWAY* MAGAZINE

*W*hile all the other homes in the quiet, hilltop town of Kalaheo, Kauai, were still dark in slumber, the residence of the Kauai Classic House (a home shared by pro bodyboarders) was a beehive of activity. Lean, tanned young men were gulping down cereal, filling gallon-size bottles of water to use as portable showers and throwing surfboards and bodyboards into the back of big, four-wheel-drive trucks.

It was a regular "dawn patrol" drill. Expert videographer and surf team coach Bob Sato scooted the "boys" into waiting cars. This contest-winning group of Christian surfers and bodyboarders (known as the Kauai Classic Team) had to get to the surf spot by the first crack of sunrise. Mike was among the crew.

Besides surfing, Mike's role within the team was to edit each day's surf footage into crisp, action-packed scenes. His experience in the sport of bodysurfing—New Zealand National Champion and fifth place in the U.S. Junior Championships—gave him a great sense for editing the sport. The team's surf spot for the day would be Major's Bay, a wave-producing arc of white sand and razor-sharp reef on the far west side of the island.

While Bob set up his video equipment under warm but overcast October skies, the rest of the guys pulled on their trunks and light wetsuit tops and readied their boards. The surf was pounding, and excitement was high.

Mike and his friends paddled out, pushing their boards deep underneath large incoming waves and popping out the back to continue the journey to get outside the place where the waves start to crest and break.

Ten minutes into the surf session, with around fifteen other surfers in the water, terror struck.

Mike saw a respectable wave stand up behind him. He slid his long frame onto his bodyboard and began to paddle hard with his arms, digging his finned feet deep into the water for speed.

It happened in an instant—and without warning. A tiger shark, estimated to be nearly fifteen feet long, shot up from the depths and clamped down hard on Mike's legs. He looked down and saw the huge greenish brown beast rise. He knew a giant shark was attacking him.

The animal was bearing down. A strong, firm pressure with accompanying dull pain shot up both legs. Mike was pulled off his board. Then the shark began to shake its gigantic frame with such violence that Mike described it as "being thrashed like a toy in a dog's mouth."

"I was determined to get this thing away from me." He bent over the monster and began to slug the shark on the head with his fist while simultaneously attempting to pull his feet from between its jaws. He was partially successful. One foot slid out and the shark twisted hard again.

Finally Mike was free. He swam to his waiting board and shot a glance at a surfer sitting only eight feet away who had witnessed the drama. The guy—not a member of the Kauai Classic team—stared at Mike with a dazed look and then paddled like a powerboat in the other direction.

The shark had torn Mike's leg off just below the calf.

Fortunately Mike didn't panic. He caught the wave and slid onto the beach without effort.

The cry "Shark attack!" spread quickly along the beach, and soon those surfing scrambled in to safety.

Having ridden on his belly to the sand, Mike attempted to stand up. "For a moment I actually forgot I had no foot," Mike explained. "But then I fell down."

Pro bodyboarder Kyle Maligro was the first one to Mike's side. Kyle quickly applied a surfboard leash to the amputated leg as a tourniquet.

Mike's injuries were extensive. In addition to the lost leg, Mike's other foot had huge gashes torn into it from being gnawed in the serrated teeth of the tiger shark. One hand also had severe wounds inflicted by the teeth, so deep that nerves and the proper use of his hand were threatened.

Blood poured over his wet body, and for a moment Mike found himself moving toward panic.

What's going to happen to me? he thought and the seed of fear began to grow. Then Kyle began to pray for him. "That," Mike said, "was the turning point."

Kyle was still praying when a four-wheel-drive truck came screaming over the sand.

In a moment, Mike found himself lying in the bed of the truck wedged between surfboards, wrapped in beach towels, and blasting over the sand toward the nearest hospital just a few miles away.

Topflight ER doctor Ken Pierce was on duty when Mike was dragged in. A surfer himself, the doc stabilized Mike and then had him transferred to a larger hospital across the island.

The thought *I'm going to get through this* went through Mike's head over and over again.

Mike's brush with a shark exploded across the tight-knit island community. Friends were so overcome with concern that they left school in the middle of class. The hospital waiting room bulged with distraught students, friends, and family. Many impromptu prayer meetings were held throughout the day.

The prayers were answered, not only by an amazing recovery, but also by the incredibly serene attitude reflected by Mike through the whole ordeal.

As the local and national press hovered around to "get the scoop,"

Mike's main comments were about how fortunate he was to be alive and how he was sure God had a reason for this accident beyond what he could imagine. Virtually every news story reported his humble, upbeat attitude.

To add irony to the situation, Mike's mangled swim fin washed ashore several days later during the filming of the story for the TV show *Hard Copy*.

When asked to reflect on what the trauma has taught him, Mike's eyes brightened.

"I learned that you really don't know how much you can trust God until something terrible happens. I never got into wondering 'why me?' but the whole thing sure made me thankful for what I do have. It has sure helped me to be able to relate to others who have suffered hardships."

On January 1, 1998, just over two months after his brush with death, Mike went surfing again. Determined not to let "worrying about some stupid shark" ruin his enjoyment of the sport he loves so much, Mike tosses his crutches up on the beach and then, with his board tucked under his arm, he hops on his good leg into the water. From that point on he's as hot as he ever was.

Today, Mike surfs every time there is a swell. He has been fitted for a prosthetic leg and is back editing videos for the Kauai Classic team. He openly talks about the shark attack as "part of something that God allowed to happen for a reason bigger than can always be figured out." And he says it with such a contagious smile that everyone knows he really believes it.

The Saint of Auschwitz

PATRICIA TREECE
ADAPTED BY MAX LUCADO
FROM *SIX HOURS ONE FRIDAY*

For all the ugly memories of Auschwitz there is one of beauty. It's the memory Gajowniczek has of Maximilian Kolbe.

In February, 1941, Kolbe was incarcerated at Auschwitz. He was a Franciscan priest. In the harshness of the slaughterhouse he maintained the gentleness of Christ. He shared his food. He gave up his bunk. He prayed for his captors. One could call him the "Saint of Auschwitz."

In July of that same year there was an escape from the prison. It was the custom at Auschwitz to kill ten prisoners for every one who escaped. All the prisoners would be gathered in the courtyard and the commandant would randomly select ten men from the ranks. These victims would be immediately taken to a cell where they would receive no food or water until they died.

The commandant begins his selection. At each selection another prisoner steps forward to fill the sinister quota. The tenth name he calls is Gajowniczek.

As the SS officers check the numbers of the condemned, one of the condemned begins to sob. "My wife and my children," he weeps.

The officers turn as they hear movement among the prisoners. The guards raise their rifles. The dogs tense, anticipating a command to attack. A prisoner has left his row and is pushing his way to the front.

It is Kolbe. No fear on his face. No hesitancy in his step. The capo shouts at him to stop or be shot. "I want to talk to the commander," he says calmly. For some reason the officer doesn't club or kill him. Kolbe stops a few paces from the commandant, removes his hat and looks the German officer in the eye.

"Herr Kommandant, I wish to make a request, please."

That no one shot him is a miracle.

"I want to die in the place of this prisoner." He points at the sobbing Gajowniczek. The audacious request is presented without stammer.

"I have no wife and children. Besides, I am old and not good for anything. He's in better condition." Kolbe knew well the Nazi mentality.

"Who are you?" the officer asks.

"A Catholic priest."

The block is stunned. The commandant, uncharacteristically speechless. After a moment, he barks, "Request granted."

Prisoners were never allowed to speak. Gajowniczek says, "I could only thank him with my eyes. I was stunned and could hardly grasp what was going on. The immensity of it: I, the condemned, am to live and someone else willingly and voluntarily offers his life for me—a stranger. Is this some dream?"

The Saint of Auschwitz outlived the other nine. In fact, he didn't die of thirst or starvation. He died only after poison was injected into his veins. It was August 14, 1941.

Gajowniczek survived the Holocaust. He made his way back to his hometown. Every year, however, he goes back to Auschwitz. Every August 14 he goes back to say thank you to the man who died in his place.

In his backyard there is a plaque. A plaque he carved with his own hands. A tribute to Maximilian Kolbe—the man who died so he could live.

Color Don't Matter

RANDY ALCORN
FROM *DOMINION*

Now, chillens, I been hearin' some talk I want to set straight. I wants you to understand not all white folks is bad. There's plenty of good ones, and don't let nobody tell you different." Obadiah spoke to his grandchildren, gathered at his request in the living room late in the afternoon. Ty sat there under protest, but Granddaddy had insisted.

"I was thirty-five when I joined the army because I wanted to serve my country. There was a private named Mike Button, from Texas. One day we was doin' field maneuvers in ninety degree heat. So we takes a break. I's standin' under a shade tree, and ol' Mike, he comes up to me and says, 'Forgot my canteen. Mind if I have a drink, Obadiah?' I reached to get my cup to pour him some water, but Mike just slaps the cup away and grabs the canteen. Then he pulls it to his mouth and takes a long draw. Well, them days whites didn't never drink from the same bottle as blacks. I knowed it weren't no accident. Mike did it on purpose. That was the beginning of a fast friendship. We wrote each other letters every Christmas until five years ago when he died. I still writes to his widow, but my hand's so shaky don't know if she can read it. One day I'm gonna see ol' Mike again because he loved Jesus and so do I. My black hand's gonna grip his white hand. And it's gonna be a strong grip then. All hell won't be able to break apart those two hands." His right eye grew heavy. He reached to it, and a big tear cascaded down his cheek.

"Tell us about the Depression, Gramps," Jonah said.

"Well, now, them were the days, I'm tellin' you. My brother Elijah, he traveled with me then. We couldn't find no work in Mississippi, so we took to ridin' the rails. We'd get off town to town, search for work all day. Most nights we was outside. We'd find some newspaper, lay it over us, and put our arms around each other jus' to keep from freezin'. Loved all my brothers and sisters, but none like ol' Elijah. And I think he'd say the same about me. One time me and 'Lijah, we was in Detroit. We was kickin' ourselves for ridin' the rail so far north, it was so cold. We was huddlin' up for the night in a back alley, and in the dark I hears someone amoanin'. So Elijah and me, we moves over to this poor man, stiff as a board. I gets on one side and Elijah on t'other, and we puts our arms around him.

"He was scared at first. Can't blame him." Obadiah laughed. "We got out of him his name was Freddy. That's the only thing he said all night. 'Frrrrrrrrrrrreddy.'" He laughed again. "Cold as ice. But after thirty minutes of his face buried in my ol' sweater, his mouth thawed out. We gived him our last piece of bread. He needed it more than we did. 'Lijah was singin' the ol' spirituals, and another hour or so Freddy got warm enough and Elijah's lullabies put him to sleep. No one could sing like Elijah. Well, come just after dawn, Elijah sings 'Amazin' Grace.' He wakes ol' Freddy up. Of course, by then we knew Freddy was white. You should've seen the look on his face when he realized he'd spent the night as lunch meat in a Negro sandwich!"

"What did he do then, Grandpa?" Jonah asked.

"Well, he stayed right there. And we got to talkin'. When it warmed up to about forty degrees, we got up and looked for work together. Became good friends. And for almost a week ol' Freddy spent the nights in that same Negro sandwich!

"Frrrrrrrrrreddy," Obadiah said again, laughing so hard it took his breath away. "I hasn't told you the best part, chillens. Freddy asked us why we cared enough to keep him warm. Me and 'Lijah, we told him the reason. It was Jesus. We went our separate ways after that week, 'cause Detroit was home for him, but if we was goin' to sleep outside, me and 'Lijah preferred Mississippi!"

"What happened to Freddy?" Keisha asked.

"Don't rightly know. Never saw him again. But one thing we learned. There's two times when color don't matter. One's when you're cold and hungry. The other's when you know Jesus."

One Rotten Day...

RACHEL SCHLABACH
FROM *CAMPUS LIFE* MAGAZINE

A *Calvin and Hobbes* cartoon on my desk says, "Some days you get up and you already know that things aren't going to go well. They're the type of days when you should give in, put your pajamas back on, make some hot chocolate, and read comic books in bed with the covers up until the world looks more encouraging."

Waking up to a thunderstorm one Monday made me feel this way. And school only made my bad mood worse. In journalism class, I'd forgotten to write story ideas for our newspaper. In geometry, I left the last page of the test blank because I'd forgotten the formula for the problems. And in history, I failed a quiz.

At the end of my horrible day, I found a note in my locker that said: "Rachel, wait for me inside the cafeteria after school. I want to talk to you. Thanks, Leslie."

What's this all about? I wondered. Leslie and I rarely talked to each other, and we weren't close friends.

When I got to the cafeteria, Leslie came to me and said, "Rachel, I know my note seemed weird, but I just wanted to tell you something...my dad left my mom last week...he just left us."

Through tearful sobs, she continued, "I really don't know why I'm telling you this, but you seem like the kind of person who cares about people."

When she stopped talking, I said slowly, "I don't know why these terrible things are happening, but I want you to know I'm willing to talk or listen, or just be around for you."

Then I talked a little about God's love, and I told her that he cared deeply about what was happening in her life. By the end of our conversation, the painful look on her face had faded a little.

As I watched her walk down the hall, I realized my so-called "rotten day" wasn't anything compared to what Leslie was facing. And I realized something else. Even when I'm in a bad mood, God may come along and say, "Stop feeling sorry for yourself! I want you to help someone today."

By the way, when I got outside, the sun was finally shining. It was like God was giving me a big smile at the end of...well, a pretty incredible Monday.

Miracle at the Mall

Joan Wester Anderson
FROM *Where Miracles Happen*

eth and Margie (not their real names), two teenage sisters, had enjoyed shopping in the large enclosed mall. But by the time they were ready to leave, it was dark. Standing at the mall exit, they could hardly see the outline of their car, the only one left in that section of the dimly lit parking lot.

The girls were nervous as they waited, hoping a few customers would come along so they could all walk out together. Both were aware of the current crime wave. There had been muggings and rapes in area shopping malls, and they remembered their father's warning: "Don't stay too late!"

"Dad's going to be furious," Beth said.

"Then we'd better get going—now!" Margie shifted her packages, pushed open the door, and walked as fast as she could. Beth followed, glancing from side to side. Street traffic had subsided, but the lot seemed a bit too quiet.

They had made it! Beth shoved the key into the car lock, got in, and reached across to open Margie's door. Just then the girls heard the sound of running feet behind them. When Margie turned around, her heart almost stopped. Racing toward them were two ominous-looking men.

"You're not going anywhere!" one shouted.

Margie screamed. Terrified, she scrambled inside, and both girls locked their doors, just in time.

With shaking fingers, Beth turned on the car's ignition switch. Nothing happened. She did it again, and again. But only the sound of the key clicked in the silence. They had no power!

"Beth, try again!" Margie was frantic. The men were pulling the door handles, pushing at the windows.

"I can't!" Beth cried. "It won't start!"

The girls knew there were only seconds of safety remaining. Quickly, they joined hands in prayer.

"Dear God," Margie pleaded, "give us a miracle!"

Once more, Beth turned the key. This time the engine roared to life. She shifted into gear and raced out of the parking lot, leaving the men behind.

The girls wept all the way home, shocked and relieved at the same time. They screeched down the driveway to the garage, stumbled into the safety of their house, and told their father what had happened. He held them both close.

"You're safe—that's the main thing," he soothed them. "But you could have been hurt or even killed. Don't ever put yourselves in that kind of situation again!"

"We won't," Margie promised, wiping her eyes.

Her father was frowning. "It's strange, though. The car has never failed to start. I'll check it out tomorrow."

Early the next morning, he raised the car's hood to look at the starter. And in one stunned glance, he realized Who had brought his daughters safely home the previous night.

For there was no battery in the car.

Belonging

My mother wasn't married when I was born so I had a hard time. When I started to go to school, my classmates had a name for me and it wasn't a very nice name. I would go off by myself at recess and during lunchtime because the taunts of my playmates cut so deeply.

What was worse was going downtown on Saturday afternoon and feeling every eye burning a hole through me. They were all wondering just who my real father was. When I was about twelve years old, a new preacher came to our church. I would always go in late and slip out early. But one day the preacher said the benediction so I got caught and had to walk out with the crowd. I could feel every eye in church on me. Just about the time I got to the door, I felt a big hand on my shoulder. I looked up and the preacher was looking right at me.

"Who are you, son? Whose boy are you?"

I felt the old weight come on me. It was like a big, black cloud. Even the preacher was putting me down.

But as he looked down at me, studying my face he began to smile a big smile of recognition. "Wait a minute," he said, "I know who you are. I see the family resemblance. You are a son of God."

With that he slapped me across the rump and said, "Boy, you've got a great inheritance. Go and claim it." That was the most important single sentence ever said to me.

When I pray, coincidences happen.
When I stop praying, coincidences stop.

—William Temple
Archbishop of Canterbury

There's Always a Reason

Missy Jenkins
as told to Kay Lawing Gupton
condensed from *Today's Christian Woman* magazine

December 1, 1997, began like any other school day—nothing out of the ordinary. My twin, Mandy, and I planned to do our homework after school, like always. Then I was going to study my driver's handbook so I could get my permit on December 24, our birthday.

Mandy and I had started our sophomore year at Heath High School with the typical classes: world civilization, algebra, journalism, English, choir, band. We'd also started going to a morning prayer group.

But at about 7:45 that morning, as our group of thirty-five students finished our devotional, a classmate, Michael Carneal, started shooting. At first, Mandy and I both thought it was a stunt. The gun pop sounded fake, like on TV. But when a bullet flew through Mandy's hair, she knew it was real. Mandy threw herself on top of me.

I'd been shot, but I didn't realize it right away. I wasn't aware of any pain, just a sensation of pressure. I felt as though I'd been knocked down. I was completely stunned, confused, in shock; I couldn't believe what had just happened. In fact, it's still unbelievable.

FAITH

After the shooting, the ambulance took me to Lourdes Hospital, near the school. The doctors told me the bullet entered my left shoulder and damaged my spinal cord. As a result, I'm paralyzed from the waist down. They told me I'll never walk again.

I was sick a lot my first week at Lourdes—nausea, fluid in my lungs, swelling around my spinal cord. Once all that improved, they started my therapy. First was the tilt table to get me used to being upright again. Then I began exercises to strengthen my arms and upper body. I also started learning how to get around in a wheelchair.

At first, dressing myself took forty-five minutes. Trying to learn how to do everything again, to be normal, was so hard it made me sick or wore me out.

Then in February, I went to Cardinal Hill Rehabilitation Hospital in Lexington, 260 miles away, to continue specialized therapy. My family went with me—my mom, Joyce; my dad, Ray; my older sister, Christie; and Mandy—and rented an apartment. I began daily physical therapy, including aerobic exercises to get my heart rate up. One of these was the arm bike, which is exactly what you would do with your feet, except it's done with your arms to strengthen them.

Another daily event was occupational therapy. There I learned how to get from my wheelchair to the bathtub, and put on my shoes.

The best of my daily therapies was recreational therapy. I got to play basketball, throw Frisbees, and swim. I also had to stand for a half hour each day, so Mandy and I would play cards to pass the time.

Thankfully, I got to leave Cardinal Hill in time to finish my sophomore year at Heath. Physical therapy continued every day—even at school. The therapists came to school at 11 A.M. to help me stretch my legs. Sitting in the wheelchair for a long time makes them stiff.

Being back at school felt comfortable because everybody treated me as though the wheelchair weren't there. Getting around in my wheelchair is more frustrating than I expected. Most places aren't wheelchair-accessible. Things that once were easy are now hard. I never even thought about them before.

I have thought about Michael and wondered why he decided to shoot us. Mandy and I both knew him; we'd been in band with him—ridden the same bus several times on trips. Joked with him. We had a lot of the same friends. Everybody knows everybody at Heath. None of us thought Michael was odd or dangerous or anything like that.

Michael took so much from so many that day. But I believe hating him is wasted emotion. I'm not the one to judge him or decide what should happen to him. It's for God to do the judging. Besides, hating Michael won't make me walk or bring my schoolmates—Kayce, Jessica, and Nicole—back to life. Their deaths still seem unreal.

Of the three, Kayce was closest to me. Every day, I think about her and the happy times we shared—parties, band, friends. I know all three are in heaven, but that doesn't keep me from missing Kayce. Nothing happens without a reason—even this—so God will somehow make good come from it. I believe that.

I do feel sorry for Michael. Unlike him, I can get on with my life. I have lots of friends supporting me every day. I'm not mad at him. I can forgive him. I would really hate the feeling of carrying an awful grudge in my heart.

A lot of people have told me my good attitude has been an inspiration to them. I think that's my purpose.

Fifth-Period Fears

ROBIN JONES GUNN
FROM *WORLDWIDE CHALLENGE* MAGAZINE

When I was in high school, I dreaded my fifth-period government class. The teacher was boring, none of my friends were in that class, and the guy who sat in front of me was a jerk. He was six feet three inches tall, had long hair, wore leather "hippie" sandals, and had a booming laugh that was almost as big as he was. Not only did Mike intimidate me, he loved to tease me, and I hated it.

I was the straight little Christian girl who didn't even go to school dances, and he was the party animal who every Monday would loudly recount his weekend escapades and then laugh when I'd blush or turn away. I hated his laugh.

I started carrying my Bible to class sometime during that semester in government. It was a paperback, *Good News for Modern Man*, and I'd made a cover for it out of pink-flowered material. A small group of Christians met at lunch time, and I provided the camouflaged Bible. We were known as the "Jesus Geeks." For such a small flock, it amazed me that other students knew who we were and why we got together. Students like Mike.

"Did you Jesus Geeks pray for me today?" Mike mocked one day when I entered government class right after lunch.

I didn't answer, but that didn't matter to him because he received the desired laughter from his friends sitting around us. I slipped into my seat and wished the teacher would hurry up and start the class.

"What's this?" Mike said, brazenly grabbing my carefully concealed Bible and thumbing through it.

I quickly tried to snatch it back, but his long arms held it over his head as he flipped through the pages and, with sudden delight, said, "Ohhh, what a pretty pink Bible! And look! It even has cute little stick figure drawings!" He showed it around to his friends, and they responded with the anticipated snickers and belittling.

Choked by humiliation, I grabbed for my Bible and spouted out the stupidest thing I'd ever said: "Why don't you just get saved and leave me alone?"

Of course that roused a wild blast of laughter from Mike and all his friends and brought enough attention to the back of the class that the teacher told us all to cool it.

With my Bible back in my quivering hands, I bravely blinked back my tears and nested my bruised treasure in my lap for the rest of the class.

The next day I wrestled with whether or not to take my Bible to school. I knew that Mike would probably use it to make fun of me some more. I don't know why, but I took it with me. At our lunch gathering I asked some of my friends to pray for me and for Mike. My friends encouraged me, and supplied me with clever comebacks and other elementary witnessing tools that I could use on Mike.

I entered government class ready for God to turn me into a bold witness. As I anticipated, Mike intercepted my Bible before I even sat down.

"Let's see what our spiritual inspiration for the day is," he spouted. Randomly opening it, he read some verse that meant nothing by itself and sounded ridiculous. His cheering section laughed and he quickly opened again to another passage and read it with his best dramatic preacher tones.

All the quick quips and sassy witnessing answers I'd been coached on escaped me. I sat frozen, as if I'd been struck dumb, feeling awful for letting the Lord down like this. I winced as Mike read another verse in his preacher tones and cracked a joke that had all his friends laughing

Unbidden, the tears came, streaking down my face. *How could this be happening?* I found absolutely no words to speak. I sat completely still, fully aware of how I must've looked—a silent, blubbering fool.

Just as Mike opened to his next random passage, he glanced at me, and his expression changed. Instead of reading another verse for laughs, he snapped my Bible shut and jokingly said something about that being enough inspiration for one day. He placed my Bible back on top of my government book. I lowered my head in shame and wiped my eyes.

When my ten-year class reunion came up, I told my husband I didn't have much interest in going. I'd only had a few friends in high school, and I hadn't dated anyone or been in any clubs. He still thought we should go since we'd missed his tenth, so we went.

The night of the reunion, I reluctantly rode with my husband in the hotel elevator to the designated floor. The doors slid open, and standing in front of the elevator was a tall, extremely good-looking man wearing an expensive suit. A beautiful blond held onto his arm.

"Robin!" The man said, wrapping his arms around me in an enthusiastic hug as I stepped out of the elevator. "I was hoping you would come!" He pulled away and, turning to the woman next to him, said, "This is the one I told you about."

My husband turned to me and whispered, "I thought you said you didn't have any boyfriends in high school?"

"I didn't!" I whispered back. "I have no idea who this guy is!"

"You don't remember me, do you?" the mysterious man asked, all smiles. "Well, I remember you, and I took your advice."

I looked at the man, then at my husband, then at the man's wife. She seemed to have suddenly made the connection. "Oh, honey," she said to him, "Is this the one who told you to get saved and leave her alone?"

He answered with a boom of rich laughter, and I knew it was Mike. After quick introductions all around, Mike told of how he had finally become a Christian during his junior year in college. "When I hit the bottom," Mike explained, "I remembered you and some of the other Jesus

Geeks from high school, and I went looking for some on my college campus. They led me to the Lord."

I cringed at the memory of my pathetic witnessing skills in high school and mumbled something about the stupid things I'd said to him in government class—how I knew I must've turned people off.

Mike laughed, and it sounded warm to me now. Gently he shook his head: "It wasn't anything you said. It was the day you cried. That day I saw something I'd never seen before: a girl in love with God. For a long time I remembered your tears because only someone who is really in love can cry like that."

Take Me Back

HEATHER FLOYD
FROM *STEADY ON...SECURED BY LOVE*

I am on a journey—an exciting, adventurous journey. It's a journey on the road of life. Along my journey I experience thrills and spills, and I encounter enormous mountains and vast valleys.

I've taken many wrong turns and a few detours, and I've lost my way in the wilderness countless times. But, somehow, I always find my way back to the road, the narrow road. God keeps it all lit up for me so I'll always be able to find my way home.

You know how on hot summer nights you can see the lights of a softball field all the way across town? Even if it's a long way off, if you'll follow the lights, you can eventually find your way to the field. God's light is like that. It penetrates the darkness and shines steadfastly, and if you'll just keep it in view and keep making your way toward it, you'll eventually end up right there with him.

But sometimes, the freedom of the wide road seems much more fun than the confines of the narrow road. And I find myself wandering off course and away from God. On the wide road, I can make my own rules and decide my own way. And I like that…for a while. But soon the air there becomes bitter and stale. And the crowds of people press against me, and I get sweaty and covered in dust. I begin to feel as if I'm suffocating. And it's so dark and I feel so lonely—even though I'm surrounded by thousands of other lost souls. And in my desperation, I begin to frantically search for the light. I finally spot it but it's far away, and I'm tired and weary. I want to give up and rest right where I am. But I know that could get me in trouble. It's sort of like sleeping in your car at a rest stop in the middle of nowhere. Anything can happen.

I'm so tired and so far from home, and I've accumulated so much baggage that I can't possibly carry it all on my own. I've been away from the light so long that I've forgotten that there are people there who really want to help, and that there is One who is strong and loving and wants to carry my load. He misses me and wants me to come home.

But I'm so ashamed. I've turned my back on Him; I can't ask Him for help now. I can't go home. Just look at me. My face is smudged with dirt, my clothes are filthy and worn, my hair is wild and out of control—just like my life. My body is covered with cuts and bruises, and I know they're there because of my own stupid choices.

I can't go home…not like this. I look again at my sad surroundings, then I lift my face to the magnificent road in the distance, all lit up and waiting for me. I know I want to go there; I want to experience the warmth of the light once again. Just then, I hear a faint noise coming from far down that luminous road. The sound gets louder and louder, and it sounds so beautiful—like someone cheering and joyfully clapping and shouting. Then I hear my name. I can't believe it. Someone is calling out my name. I begin to walk forward so I can hear better, and before long, I'm running so fast I can't stop. The voice is so familiar. Finally, I see where it's coming from. It's the most glorious vision I've ever seen. A crowd of people, shouting my name and cheering me on—some I recognize and some I don't—but all of them are cheering just for me. And when they see me, they cheer even louder, as if I'm about to score a winning run.

Then I see Him. His face is shining, and His eyes are locked onto mine. I know Him at once. He's my Creator, my Savior, He doesn't wait for me to reach Him, but He runs to me and embraces me with tears flooding His face.

I'm home! I'm home! And I'm surrounded by the ones I love most—precious people who have interceded on my behalf to our Creator and with their prayers created a hedge of protection around me that nothing could penetrate.

Have you ever taken a detour on the journey of life? Have you strayed from the narrow road and been enticed by the sights and sounds of the masses? Have you lost your way and felt you could never find your way back home? We've all been there. We've all strayed. We've all wandered off the path. But your story can end just like mine. The road to your loving heavenly Father is always lit, and you are always welcome on it. There are people there who are cheering you on, even now, and there is a Savior who waits longingly for you to turn your face toward home. When you take those first steps toward home, He'll run to meet you.

It's so easy to get distracted and turn from the path God has laid out for us. And when we find ourselves in those dark places, we do things we wouldn't want anyone to see. If the light were turned on our sin, we would be horrified. If ever you find yourself doing something you wouldn't want the people you respect to know about, a loud alarm should sound in your head and warn you to stop! But God does see everything we do. Imagine living in a house of mirrors. Everywhere you look, there you are. Everything you do, you see yourself do. God is our house of mirrors. Everywhere we go, He goes. Everything we do, He sees. Everything we say, He hears.

The challenge is to remain constantly aware and mindful of His presence and to keep our feet planted firmly on His path. Because I carry the name of Christ, I am called to live by a higher standard. I will never be like Him completely, but I will strive to be more like Him every day.

And if I stray, He faithfully waits for me at the end of the well-lit road.

There is a time for everything,

and a season for every activity under heaven;

A time to be born and a time to die...

A time to weep and a time to laugh.

Ecclesiastes 3:1–2, 4

Send us your stories for More Stories for a Teen's Heart

We would love to have you submit a story or a quote for our next book for teenagers.

If you don't write the story yourself, please send us as much information as you can about where you found it—things like the name and address of author, name of the book or magazine, date it was published, page number, publisher, and any other information you have. We will credit both you and the original author.

If you write the story yourself, please give us a little information about who you are and what you do.

If you send us something, we will not be able to acknowledge receiving it but promise to contact you if we are going to use it in one of the books in the *Stories for the Heart* series. It is not necessary to send a self-addressed stamped envelope, but be sure to include your name, address, and phone number.

Send stories and quotes to:

Multnomah Publishers, Inc.
Stories for the Heart
P.O. Box 1720
Sisters, Oregon 97759

Acknowledgments

More than a thousand books and magazines were researched for this collection as well as a review of hundreds of stories sent by friends and readers of the *Stories of the Heart* collection. A diligent search has been made to trace original ownership, and when necessary, permission to reprint has been obtained. If I have overlooked giving proper credit to anyone, please accept my apologies. If you will contact Multnomah Publishers, Inc., Post Office Box 1720, Sisters, Oregon 97759, corrections will be made prior to additional printings.

Notes and acknowledgments are listed by story title in the order they appear in each section of the book. For permission to reprint any of the stories please request permission from the original source listed below. Grateful acknowledgment is made to authors, publishers, and agents who granted permission for reprinting these stories.

FAMILY

"Love's Sacrifice," by Kathi Kingma. Used by permission of the author.

"Prom Date," by Sean Covey. Reprinted with the permission of Simon & Schuster Inc. from THE 7 HABITS OF HIGHLY EFFECTIVE TEENS by Sean Covey. © 1998 by Franklin Covey Co.

"Grandma's Gift," by Wayne Rice. Taken from MORE HOT ILLUSTRATIONS FOR YOUTH TALKS by Wayne Rice. © 1995 by Youth Specialties, Inc. Used by permission of Zondervan Publishing House.

"Not All Valentines Come in Envelopes," by Robin Jones Gunn. Used by permission of the author. Bestselling author of over forty-five books including MOTHERING BY HEART and the Glenbrooke Series by Multnomah Publishers, and the Christy Miller Series.

"Stick Shift," by Clark Cothern. Taken from AT THE HEART OF EVERY GREAT FATHER by Clark Cothern. © 1998. Used by permission of Multnomah Publishers, Inc.

"Love Letters to My Unborn Child," by Judith Hayes. Used by permission of the author. My "Love Letters" story came from the heart of a young mother to be. I had a very sad childhood, but I was determined from the start to express my love for my children. Sasha is now a Pediatric R.N. and happily married.

"Christmas Day in the Morning," by Pearl S. Buck, Harold Ober Associates, 1955. Used by permission.

INSPIRATION

"The Blind Bomber," Reprinted with the permission of Simon & Schuster Books for Young Readers, an imprint of Simon & Schuster Children's Publishing Division from THE GREATEST SPORTS STORIES NEVER TOLD by Bruce Nash & Allan Zullo. © 1993 Nash & Zullo Productions, Inc.

"For My Sister," by David C. Needham from CLOSE TO HIS MAJESTY (Sisters, Oregon, Multnomah Books, a division of Multnomah Publishers, Inc., 1987). Used by permission.

"Maria's New Shoes," by Mary-Pat Hoffman. Original source unknown.

Cartoon by Rick Stromoski, Humorously illustrating, rstromoski @aol.com. Used by permission.

"More Out of Life," by Joe White. Excerpt taken from OVER THE EDGE AND BACK by Joe White. © 1992. Used by permission of the author.

"A Christmas Gift I'll Never Forget," by Linda DeMers Hummel. Reprinted with permission from the December 1994 *Reader's Digest* and the author. Originally printed in *Family Circle* magazine.

FRIENDS

"Sunshine," by Sarah Wood. Reprinted from "Friends," edited by Carl Koch, Saint Mary's Press, Winona, MN. Used with permission of the publisher. All rights reserved. Used with permission of the author.

"Annie," by Samantha Ecker. Reprinted from "Friends," edited by Carl Koch, Saint Mary's Press, Winona, MN. Used with permission of the publisher. All rights reserved. Used with permission of the author.

"The Green-Eyed Monster," by Teresa Cleary. Excerpt taken from WWJD STORIES FOR TEENS by Karen DeSollar. Honor Books, Tulsa, OK, © 1998. Reprinted by permission.

"You Did More Than Carry My Books," by John W. Schlatter.

"Downhill Race," by Shaun Schwartz. An earlier version of "Downhill Race" by Shaun Schwartz appeared in TREASURES 2: STORIES & ART BY STUDENTS IN OREGON, edited by Chris Weber and published by the Oregon Students Writing and Art Foundation, © 1988. Reprinted by permission.

"My Name is Ike," by Gary Paulsen. Excerpt taken from MY LIFE IN DOG YEARS. Dell Publishing © 1998 by Gary Paulsen.

"Diamonds," by Irene Sola'nge McCalphin. Reprinted from "Friends," edited by Carl Koch, Saint Mary's Press, Winona, MN. Used with permission of the publisher. All rights reserved. Used with permission of the author.

"The Friendly Rival," by Bruce Nash & Allan Zullo. Reprinted with the permission of Simon & Schuster Books for Young Readers, an imprint of Simon & Schuster Children's Publishing Division from THE GREATEST SPORTS STORIES NEVER TOLD by Bruce Nash and Allan Zullo. © 1993 Nash & Zullo Productions, Inc.

"What's the Big Deal?" by Julie Berens. Excerpt from WWJD STORIES FOR

ENCOURAGEMENT

inspirational speaker who focuses on developing creative connections between women and God. Renie and her husband, Robert, recently celebrated twenty-seven years of marriage. They are parents to Holly and Heather and live in Schaumberg, Illinois, with their two neurotic cats. Contact: creativeconnections@ibm.net.

Cartoon by Rick Stromoski, Humorously illustrating, rstromoski@aol.com. Used by permission.

"All Changes Begin With You," by Sean Covey. Reprinted with the permission of Simon & Schuster, Inc. from THE 7 HABITS OF HIGHLY EFFECTIVE TEENS by Sean Covey. © 1998 by Franklin Covey.

"A Basket of Love," by Chris A. Wolff. A condensed version of this article appeared in the March/April 1999 issue of the *Christian Reader.* For reprint permission please contact Chris Wolff at 3045 S. Archibald Ave. Ste. H, PMB # 303, Ontario, CA 91761.

GOOD TIMES

"We Would Have Danced All Night," by Guy Rice Doud. Excerpt taken from MOLDER OF DREAMS by Guy Rice Doud, a Focus on the Family book published by Tyndale House. © 1990 by Guy Doud. All rights reserved. International copyright secured. Used by permission.

"Tori's Last Chance," by Jeannie St. John Taylor. Used by permission of the author.

"For the Love of Strangers," by Robin Jones Gunn. Used by permission of the author. All rights retained. Reprinted from *Virtue* magazine, Sep/Oct. 1989.

"Driving Lessons," from *The Grace Awakening* by Charles Swindoll, © 1990, Word Publishing, Nashville, TN. All rights reserved.

"Dream Date," by Larry Anderson. Excerpt taken from TAKING THE TRAUMA OUT OF TEEN TRANSITIONS by Larry Anderson © 1991. Used by permission of the author.

"Magical Moments," by Rhonda Marcks. Used by permission of the author.

"Of More Value," by Jerry B. Jenkins. Excerpt taken from STILL THE ONE by Jerry B. Jenkins, a Focus on the Family book published by Tyndale House. © 1995 by Jerry B. Jenkins. All rights reserved. International copyright secured. Used by permission.

"The New Kid." Excerpted from MORE RANDOM ACTS OF KINDNESS by the editors of Conari Press, © 1998 by the editors of Conari Press, by permission of Conari Press.

"In the Dugout," by Jack Eppolito. From *Christian Reader* (July/August 1996). Used by permission.

"Live!" by Emily Campagna. Used by permission of author. Quoted from her high school graduation speech, Mountain View High Scool, 1999.

"Seeing Each Other in a Different Light," by Susan Manegold. Used by permission of author. Originally printed in *Women's World* magazine.

MAKING A DIFFERENCE

"Goodwill," by Cynthia Hamond. Taken from CHICKEN SOUP FOR KIDS. Used by permission of the author.

"Little Lies," by Meredith Proost. An earlier version of "Little Lies" by Meredith Proost appeared in TREASURES: STORIES & ART BY STUDENTS IN OREGON, edited by Chris Weber and published by the Oregon Students Writing & Art Foundation, © 1985. Reprinted with permission.

"Standing Tall," by Steve Farrar. Excerpt taken from STANDING TALL by Steve Farrar, Multnomah Books, Sisters, OR, © 1994. Used by permission.

"I Should Have Said Something..." by Christy Simon. Reprinted from *Campus Life* magazine (March/April 1998). © 1998. Christina M. Simon, a *Campus Life* contributing writer, is a senior at the University of Evansville (Evansville, Indiana), where she is editor-in-chief of the campus newspaper, *The Crescent*. Used by permission of the author.

"Call Me," by Cynthia Hamond. © 1998. Used by permission of author.

"Dump Boy," by Philip Gulley. Excerpt taken from HOME TOWN TALES by Philip Gulley, Multnomah Publishers, Inc., Sisters, OR, © 1998. Used by permission.

"Are You Wondering Where Your Son Is?" by Tim Hansel. Excerpt taken from WHAT KIDS NEED MOST IN A DAD by Tim Hansel, Fleming H. Revell, a division of Baker Book House Company, © 1984. Used by permission.

"The Winning Check." Excerpt taken from GOD'S LITTLE DEVOTIONAL BOOK. Honor Books, Inc. Tulsa, OK, © 1995. Used by permission.

"Yerr Out!" by Clark Cothern. Excerpt taken from AT THE HEART OF EVERY GREAT FATHER by Clark Cothern, Multnomah Publishers, Inc., Sisters, OR, © 1998. Used by permission.

"Foolproof," by Alan Cliburn. Excerpt taken from WWJD STORIES FOR TEENS by Karen DeSollar. Harbor Books, Tulsa, OK, © 1998. Used by permission.

"The Toolbox," by Joshua Harris. Excerpt taken from I KISSED DATING GOODBYE by Joshua Harris, Multnomah Publishers, Inc., Sisters, OR, © 1997. Used by permission.

"The Joy Ride," by Suzy Ryan. © 1999. Suzy Ryan lives with her family in southern California. Used by permission of the author.

"Making Sarah Cry," by Cheryl L. Costello-Forshey. Used by permission of author.

CHANGING

"Eighth Grade Bully," by Mike Buetelle. Used by permission of the author.

"Wake-up Call," by Bob Welch. Excerpt taken from A FATHER FOR ALL

SEASONS by Bob Welch. © 1998 by Bob Welch. Published by Harvest House Publishers, Eugene, OR 97402. Used by permission.

"The Story Teller," author and original source unknown. Quoted from Real magazine.

"Full Circle," by Janna L. Graber. © 1997. Janna Graber is a freelance journalist who writes for the Chicago Tribune, Family Circle, Moms on Call, and numerous other magazines. Contact her at: janna.graber@reporters.net. Used by permission of the author.

"My Own Rainbow," by Randi Curtiss. Excerpt taken from WHERE THE HEART IS compiled by Chick Moorman. Personal Power Press, Saginaw, MI, © 1996. Used by permission of the author.

"Curse or Blessing," by Max Lucado. Excerpt taken from IN THE EYE OF THE STORM by Max Lucado, © 1991, Word Publishing, Nashville, Tennessee. All rights reserved.

"She's Seventeen," by Gloria Gaither. Excerpt taken from LET'S MAKE A MEMORY by Gloria Gaither & Shirley Dobson, © 1983, Word Publishing, Nashville, Tennessee. All rights reserved.

"Dad," author and original source unknown.

"The Signal," retold by Alice Gray. Taken from a familiar story passed down from my mother and others.

"The Riddle," author unknown. As cited in MORE OF...THE BEST OF BITS AND PIECES. Published by the Economics Press, Inc., 12 Daniel Rd., Fairfield, NJ 07004; 1-800-526-2554; Web site www.epinc.com. © 1997, pg. 87.

"A Blue Ribbon," author and original source unknown.

"Choices," by Sara Ann Zinn. Used by permission of the author.

"Best Friends," by Alicia M. Boxler. Used by permission of the author.

FAITH

"Kevin's Different World," by Kelly Adkins. Taken from Campus Life magazine (January/February 1999). Used by permission of the author.

"How Sweet the Sound," by Cynthia Hamond. © 1999. Used by permission of the author.

"The Bullet," by Doris Sanford. © 1997. Used by permission of the author. Doris Sanford is the author of twenty-nine books and is a consultant for a statewide program for abused children.

"Shark Attack!" by Rick Bundschuh. Taken from Breakaway magazine (July 1998). Used by permission of the author.

"The Saint of Auschwitz," by Patricia Treece. This story is adapted from the book A MAN FOR OTHERS by Patricia Treece. Published by Harper San Francisco and Marytown Press, © 1982. Used by permission of the author. Quoted from SIX HOURS ONE FRIDAY by Max Lucado. (Multnomah Publishers, Inc.).